P9-CQK-829

WORDS OF PRAISE FOR TIME TRAPS, BY TODD DUNCAN

"A primary reason why salespeople aren't successful is that *they don't spend enough time selling*. They stay busy, but they aren't productive. *Time Traps* offers a ready solution.

Sales expert Todd Dunan shows you have to use your time rather than abuse it. He'll teach you to make time an ally to become productive and prosperous. Make time to read this book."

> — **Mark Sanborn**
> Author, *The Fred Factor: How Passion
> in Your Work and Life Can Make the
> Ordinary Extraordinary*
> President, Sanborn & Associates, Inc., an
> idea studio for leadership development

"If you've not read anything by Todd Duncan, you're missing out on making a lot more sales. Most salespeople are frustrated that there never seems to be enough time to do all that they intend to and have accepted that as their lot in life. Duncan knows what it takes to get the most out of a day, and you would be all the wiser for heeding his advice in *Time Traps*. It's a career- and life-changing book."

> — **John C. Maxwell**
> *New York Times* best-selling author of
> *The 21 Irrefutable Laws of Leadership*

"When Todd Duncan writes to salespeople, you better pay close attention. *Time Traps* is his latest work and is the best material ever written on the topic. Come to think of it, you don't even have to be in sales to gain from Todd's solid advice."

> — **Pat Williams**
> Senior Vice President, Orlando Magic

"Never in this fast-moving world, when workaholism has become chic and our jobs have usurped our identities, have sales professionals needed a message more timely than Todd Duncan's *Time Traps*. This book is a must for every salesperson in America."

> — **Andy Andrews**
> Author of the *New York Times* bestseller,
> *The Traveler's Gift*.

"*Time Traps* shows you in proven fashion that it is very possible to be highly successful in the sales profession without working yourself to death. This is a must read for anyone who is tired of being swamped."

> — **Laurie Beth Jones**
> Author of *Jesus CEO*, *The Path*,
> and *Jesus, Life Coach*

"This practical, powerful book shows you how to set goals, select priorities, and double or triple your sales—almost overnight!"

— **Brian Tracy**
Author, *Million Dollar Habits* and
Time Power

"Todd Duncan has a gift for recognizing the burdens and challenges of success-oriented people. This book is once again right on target as a *lifesaver* for many struggling and talented professionals, who just need some practical help as they seek to have a life while they are making a living. Sales professionals, business owners, and executives of all kinds will find this fresh advice and wisdom immensely useful and liberating. I will recommend the book immediately to everyone I know."

— **Jim Dornan**
President and Founder of Network 21,
and coauthor of *Becoming a Person of
Influence* (with John Maxwell)

"In *Time Traps,* Mr. Duncan captures with powerful images the 'traps' that waste our time and diminish our productivity. He then suggests how to avoid those traps and to manage our daily tasks, thus increasing productivity and improving our sense of self. A fascinating read."

— **Hyrum Smith**
Vice Chairman of the Board of
FranklinCovey

"Don't waste another second reading these quotes! Open this book and start learning how to expand your business without sacrificing your life."

— **Gary Keller**
Author, *The Millionaire Real Estate
Agent*

TIME
TRAPS

PROVEN STRATEGIES FOR
SWAMPED SALESPEOPLE

TODD M. DUNCAN

OLIVER
NELSON

NELSON BOOKS
A Division of Thomas Nelson Publishers
Since 1798
www.thomasnelson.com

Published in Nashville, Tennessee, by Thomas Nelson, Inc.

Nelson Books may be purchased in bulk for educational, business, fundraising, or sales promotional use. For information, please email SpecialMarkets@ThomasNelson.com.

Library of Congress Cataloging-in-Publication Data

Duncan, Todd, 1957–
 Time traps : proven strategies for swamped salespeople / Todd M. Duncan.
  p. cm.
 Includes bibliographical references.
 ISBN 0-7852-6323-3 (hardcover)
 1. Sales management. 2. Time management. I. Title.
HF5438.4.D857 2004
658.8'1—dc22   2004023129

Printed in the United States of America

05 06 07 08 QW 5 4

THE ONLY TIME THAT COUNTS IS THE TIME
THAT YOU MAKE COUNT. TIME MATTERS, TODAY
MATTERS—MAKE IT YOUR MASTERPIECE!

Contents

CONTENTS

Chapter One

Chasing the Wind

Wasting Time Managing Time

All work contains drudgery; the issue is whether it holds meaning or not.

—WENDELL BERRY

You can't eat for eight hours a day, nor drink for eight hours a day—all you can do for eight hours is work. Which is the reason man makes himself and everybody so miserable and unhappy.

—WILLIAM FAULKNER

T im couldn't believe it. Actually, he was disgusted. *Those numbers couldn't be right.* He punched them into the calculator one more time. Three hundred thirty-six hours, divided by eight-hour days, equals . . . forty-two days. It *was* right. No, it was *frustrating*.

When Tim tallied the amount of time he had stood at the fax machine over the course of the previous year, that's what it amounted to: 336 hours inserting fax paper, fishing out jammed faxes, gazing at flashing fax numbers, waiting for fax confirmations, and refaxing misfaxes. Divided into eight-hour increments, that meant he had spent forty-two days standing over a fax machine. It would have been more amusing if it had not been so telling. The bitter truth was that Tim had literally faxed away one-fifth of his work year. Now he wondered what else he had wasted his time on. Making copies? How much time had he spent on that? And what about stapling? He probably had spent thirty days stapling paperwork and another ten days removing staples. Okay, maybe that was going a bit far, but at the very least he knew that if he could spend forty-two workdays faxing, chances were good that he was wasting most of his selling time doing menial tasks. And that raised the most aggravating question of all: How much more successful *would he be* if he didn't waste so much time? Maybe he could at least take a vacation, something he hadn't done in a while.

I bet you have been in a similar place, wondering what more you could accomplish if you weren't so busy. Wishing there was a way to slow down life and speed up business simultaneously. Well, I want you to know something: there is a way, and it's not by practicing better time management. In fact, I think time management is a waste of your time. It's like chasing the wind.

Time management is a waste of your time. It's like chasing the wind.

You see, the notion that we can manage something that is unchanging and fixed is somewhat fanciful. You can't manage or tame or control time any more than you can lasso the wind and tie it to a fence post. Yet for years that's been the gist of nearly every solution we've been given to help us deal with the incessant demands and busyness that seem unavoidable as sales professionals. *Just manage your time better; that'll do the trick.* But it hasn't done the trick, has it? Despite our best efforts, we still show up late to meetings, forget appointments, skip lunch, miss dinner, work weekends, and in general, get downright swamped. If I gave you five minutes right now, you could probably think of five things you won't get done today.

It's overwhelming, isn't it?

And here's why.

THE TRUTH ABOUT TIME

We measure the value of time by how we spend it. "How was your weekend?" a friend asks. "Wonderful," you respond, "I had a great time." In another instance your spouse inquires about how your meeting went. "Terrible," you reply. "It was a complete waste of time." It's a safe bet that if you spent a day doing something you enjoyed or that produced a desired result, you felt the day was good. On the other hand, if you spent the majority of a day doing something you didn't enjoy or that didn't produce a desired result, you probably felt the day was bad. Therefore, "rich," as my son Matthew reminded me the other day, "is not about money; rich is about *life*." And *life* is made up of one thing: time.

Matthew probably doesn't realize how much wisdom he speaks, but that's because he's only seven years old. He hasn't yet experienced a day that begins with a 7:00 AM department meeting, followed by an 8:00 AM conference call, followed by a 9:00 AM face-to-face appointment, followed by the discovery of seventeen new e-mails, eight new voice mails, and a leftover to-do list that will run into next week. And that's all before lunch. One day Matthew will realize that a kid's life is truly an enviable existence, because time is in great supply, and life is, therefore, full of possibility. But I pray that he never loses the wisdom of the truth he speaks, because growing up doesn't have to change one's view of time.

Unfortunately, it often does.

Most days, time takes more life from us than we take from it. And it's obviously not because we enjoy being stressed and frustrated and full of regret; it's because time is consistently more consistent than we are. Time is predetermined, set in perpetual motion by God "in the beginning"[1] and there is no slowing its pace or altering its consistency. That's why managing time is a bit unrealistic.

The notion of time management is not just a play on words either. It represents a flawed understanding of time that affects how we react to our time frustrations. These busy days require a new solution—one that takes into account the fact that we cannot manage the clock; we can only manage our thoughts and actions.

We cannot manage the clock; we can only manage our thoughts and actions.

I know you're very busy. That's why I am very grateful that you have generously given me part of your day. In return, I will do my best to offer you some fresh solutions to your time struggles, a liberating message that will not only teach you how to sell more while working less, but will also show you how to live more while regretting less. I know it may sound like an empty promise, and if I were hearing this for the first time, I might be skeptical too. But I've witnessed too many salespeople turn their businesses and lives around by changing both their understanding of time and their treatment of time problems. Remember our faxing friend, Tim? He was one of them.

As a result of applying the time principles and practices you will read about in this book, Tim now sells $80 million in home loans by working about eighty days a year. Yes, only eighty days a year. Once a workaholic logging seventy-plus-hour weeks, he's now an enigma in a world where late nights and long hours are fashionable and seem necessary. Yet Tim holds no secrets or special powers. He's no different from you or me. He's just an ordinary salesperson who came to understand a little something about time—and it transformed his business and life. What he learned and is reaping are what this book is all about.

But let's get real honest first.

TIME MATTERS . . . ALL THE TIME

You could hear the wind screaming past the open door. My executive team and I were two and a half miles above the earth, and it was time to jump. The man standing by the large opening in the plane's side shouted over the noise. On zero, you couldn't hesitate. We had practiced on the ground all day long, we had studied how to jump and what to expect, our packs were secure and tightly fastened, and we had donned our helmets. Now it was go time. We were as ready as we were gonna be. The four of us smacked our hands together and hollered in out-of-character fashion the way guys do when they're nervous. "Three—two—one—Go!" One by one we dropped from the plane like bombs from a B-52 and sped toward the ground at 120 miles per hour. Now, whether we liked it or not, our lives were in our own hands. The time we spent on the ground learning and planning and rehearsing was gone. All that mattered now were the next sixty seconds. We had to pay attention to the time; it was real important—life-or-death important. To pull the rip cord too early would endanger a fellow skydiver and could send you off course. To pull the cord too late was, well, far worse. Time really matters in those moments, and I was aware of each passing second.

Sheryl and I recently chartered a dive boat with a group of friends and toured some of the best dive spots around the Fijian islands. One morning we were on a deepwater dive to view several species of sharks. When we reached the bottom of the canyon, I glanced at my computer, and it read 120 feet. I remember peering up toward the surface and the surreal feeling that I was twelve stories from safety. When you're that far below the surface and you know that you only have a certain amount of air, and that once you start to ascend, you can only rise at 15 feet every five minutes, you have to pay attention to the time. If you ascend too late, you will run out of oxygen. Too fast and you'll get the bends, which can kill you just as quick. In such moments, time matters a lot, so my flippers didn't sweep the water once without much deliberation.

When is your next vacation? Chances are good that as the date for your departure nears, you will become more purposeful about your time. You will say no to things that you'd normally say yes to. You will become more efficient about getting things done because you know that if you don't, your vacation won't be relaxing. Time matters in moments like these because the return is immediate. It's bewildering how we treat our time: in one instance, we seem at peace with its passing; in another instance, we squander it miserably and regret every moment. It's a hypocrisy that, oddly enough, offers some hope.

BEHIND THE TIMES

It would seem by the way most of us act that time only matters in critical or cost-effective moments. In other words, by the way we run our lives (and careers) time only seems to matter (1) *when it has to*—like when you're two miles above the earth or 120 feet below the surface of the ocean . . . or about to get fired if you don't make a sale; or (2) *when it offers immediate rewards*—like when you're about to go on vacation . . . or when you're vying for a big account. We seem very adept at making our time count in these moments, don't we? Yet in all the other moments of which our lives are made, we seem to have great difficulty putting together ten productive minutes in a row—especially when it comes to our jobs.

The truth is that it wouldn't be so frustrating if we didn't know we could do better. And that, ironically, is our hope. We know we can *do* better because in some instances we have *done* better.

The fact that we have paid close attention to time and valued every second at some point in our lives—even if it was just before vacation or just after we jumped out of a plane—proves that we have the know-how and capacity to make time matter. The problem lies in the obstacles that keep us from doing it more often. I call the obstacles *time traps,* and our lives as salespeople are full of them.

DON'T SURRENDER

Trying to beat the time traps that seem omnipotent in the sales profession can be a frustrating thing. Most salespeople just give up and accept an existence in which chaos is part of the status quo. Marcia Hornok summed up the act of surrender this way:

Psalm 23, Antithesis

The clock is my dictator, I shall not rest.
It makes me lie down only when exhausted.
It leads me to deep depression, it hounds my soul.
It leads me in circles of frenzy for activity's sake.
Even though I run frantically from task to task,
I will never get it all done, for my "ideal" is with me.
Deadlines and my need for approval, they drive me.
They demand performance from me, beyond the limits of my schedule.
They anoint my head with migraines, my in-basket overflows.
Surely fatigue and time pressure shall follow me all the days of my life,
And I will dwell in the bonds of frustration forever.[2]

We laugh because we can empathize. But who wants to live in the "bonds of frustration forever"? I know that's not how we want to feel, because we experience guilt when we are wasting time and delight when we are spending time well.

Think about the last time you spent a wonderful evening with one of your favorite people doing one of your favorite things. Wasn't it refreshing and uplifting? Didn't you feel alive? We want more times like that, don't we?

Now think about the last time you squandered a half hour looking for your keys. How'd that feel? Not good, huh? Frustrating, to say the least. Unnerving is more accurate. Now think about how it felt when you showed up late for the event you were headed to before you realized you'd lost your keys. How did you feel then? Guilty, probably. You were almost certainly overly apologetic. Wasting time feels bad, no matter how you waste it. And as salespeople, we feel bad more often than we feel good. The solution is to work in such a way that the opposite is true. And it can be done, in more ways that one.

> *Wasting time feels bad, no matter how you waste it.*

Depending on your particular area(s) of inefficiency and frustration, there are specific and immediate actions you can take to reposition your business and subsequently your life to a place where the majority of your time is delightfully well spent—a world of time freedom—an existence not unlike my son Matthew's (only, with some responsibilities).

You may not find yourself in every trap we discuss. That doesn't mean it's not still out there, waiting to steal your time and energy. With such traps, education and avoidance are your best defense. Therefore, in the chapters that speak directly to your struggles, apply the solution to step out of the trap and experience some freedom. In the chapters that don't quite apply to your struggles, safeguard your future days by learning how to sidestep the trap.

The Toughest Challenge in Sales

Time can be a frustrating thing, especially in a profession where most of it is shared with customers who often have their own agendas. However, selling is our career of choice, so we have a battle to fight—and though it often feels like an uphill battle, it's not a lost cause.

Every salesperson has a challenge with time. It is the most repetitive and pervasive problem I've come across in fifteen years of sales training, and it doesn't just go away. The details of our stories may be different—some of us struggle every day, and others only now and then—but the results are predictably similar. What didn't get done overflows to tomorrow. What was meant for tomorrow gets reshuffled to the next day or the next week. To-do lists never get done on the day for which they were intended. Post-it Notes lose their stickiness, and the dream of productivity fades into a very real state of busyness and urgency.

In one way or another, we all are trapped by the relentless, ever-diminishing nature of time, and we often feel doomed to work more than we should to accomplish less than we could. In sum, we are frustrated that there never seems to be enough hours to do all that we intend to do. Most salespeople have accepted this as their lot in life, but you will soon see that it is not the way it has to be. I have many stories to prove it.

Changing Times

It was a first in my career as a speaker. The man approached me as I prepared to speak and handed me a five-page note. He looked at me with wide, glassy eyes and said, "Thank you." Sensing the significance of the moment, I opened the note immediately. My eyes first went to the top corner of the page, where he had recorded the hour and date. It was written at four o'clock that morning.

My heart welled up as I noticed the dried splotches of blue ink that stained the page. This was no ordinary thank-you. Then one paragraph said it all:

> The tears are from the joy of knowing that over the last year I have received more business than I ever dreamed possible; but more importantly, I have a life. I am more balanced than ever and cannot describe adequately for you how this new view on time has changed my life forever.

For fifteen years, this is all I have attempted to do. I have strived to help sales professionals realize that there is a better way to work and live—and it has everything to do with time. As I pore over the binders of letters I have saved, I am struck by how critical it is to convey in these opening pages that you *can* be highly successful in sales without working yourself to death and sacrificing all the other things that are important to you. The people whose testimonies I am reading are no different from you or me; work took up most, if not all, of their days. But with some encouragement and a new perspective, all of them turned their lives around; and I know you can too. As you turn the pages of this book, let the echo of their words give you hope that things can and soon will improve.

"It's 6:18 AM. For months I have pounded excuses into my head as to why I have been unable to accomplish what you teach. But what I once thought was impossible is now a reality."

"You literally saved my life when no one else would have been strong enough or have cared enough or have known enough to do it."

"Drinking, after a few years, started to consume my life. I didn't know my wife or my children, and I was in trouble. Then I read your book— what a life-changing event . . . I was so excited that after three chapters, I quit reading it. That was all it took . . . I quit drinking and started planning the rest of my life. My wife and kids gave me another chance. I never dreamed that marriage and being a dad could be this good. And business has never been better."

"In light of his death, I find great satisfaction in knowing he spent his four years as a husband and one month as a father putting his family ahead of his work. As busy as he was, he would leave the office every day at 5:30, knowing he was leaving for something more important. For this I thank you."

"I can't believe I let myself slide to such a low level . . . My days had become so dysfunctional and nonproductive that I was going home every night with a bad attitude that I always justified as a product of my daily stresses. I spent my days reacting to problems and not doing the important stuff. At the end of the day I always seemed to have two choices: neglect my work and go home, or neglect my family and do the work I should have done all day. I would generally go home, but angrily, because I had no sense of peace about the loose ends I was leaving at work . . . Two years have now passed since your seminar, and my business is totally under control. Recently I asked my wife to answer a question: How do you feel about me? I've sent you a copy." *(His wife handwrote an eight-page letter that gushed with love, admiration, praise, and appreciation for her husband.)*

"I must tell you that I was in no way prepared for how deeply you and your teachings would touch my soul. The insight you have given me—about me—is incredible. Thank you so much for taking the time to identify and clarify the very critical, yet often real, success."

In what ways are you frustrated as a salesperson? What circumstances would you like to change in your job and your life? Where are you missing out? Chances are good that all your answers have something to do with how you are spending (or not spending) your time.

As we embark on this journey together, I want you to know that my motivation for writing springs from my commitment and resolve to make a difference in your life—not just your business. I want to help you set yourself free from the traps that sap your best energy and steal your most precious commodity on and off the job. I want to help you live the life that you may have written off as impossible. Because it is possible, you know. And I'll show you how.

Executive Summary

Every salesperson has a challenge with time. It is the most repetitive and pervasive problem I've come across in fifteen years of sales training, and it doesn't just go away. The details of our stories may be different, but the result is predictably similar. In one way or another, most of us feel trapped by the relentless, ever-diminishing nature of time, and we often feel doomed to work more than we should to accomplish less than we could. Most salespeople have accepted this as their lot in life, but that is not the way it has to be.

Until now, most of the advice we've been offered to remedy this frustration is encompassed in the term time management. Unfortunately, as I said before, time management is a waste of your time. It's like chasing the wind.

Since we measure the value of time by how we spend it, task management is the real solution to our overly busy lives. It's the only way to get yourself out of the swamped state in which you find yourself so often.

There are specific, immediate actions you can take to shift your business and consequently your life to a place where most of your time is well spent—a world of time freedom. In each chapter I will present these proven solutions to you as the antithesis of the most common struggle that prohibits salespeople from applying it to their lives. I call them time traps, and our lives as salespeople are full of them. Take the Identity Trap . . .

Chapter Two

The Identity Trap
Wasting Time Losing Yourself

In a quintessential American way, being busy, being overworked conveys status and self-worth.

—AL GINI

To say a man holds a job is to mistake the fact. The job holds the man.

—JAMES GOULD COZZENS

As children, we wanted to be some*thing*—a ballplayer, a ballerina, a doctor, a nurse, a lawyer, a teacher. We had all the time in the world to dream, and so we did. As teens we wanted to be some*one*. We were each the same something—a student—so what mattered most was acceptance, who we were seen to be. Popularity was more important than our place in the world. But then, sometime after high school, our wantings began to merge into a grander vision for our lives. We wanted to be both some*thing* and some*one*. And at the heart of that vision was a job.

There's something seductive about your first real job, say authors Barrie Greiff and Preston K. Munter: "Young executives experience a high . . . The title, the assistant, lunches with the [bosses], the sense of power, the heady feeling of associating with the affluent—there is something . . . quickly addicting about all of this."[1] For most of us it is the first time we *welcome* responsibility, because with the responsibility of a job comes a sense of control over one's life and, for once, a sense of identity that doesn't have to do with our families or friends. With a professional job, we are given the power to determine who we are and who people see us to be.

One's first job is a chance to "make something of oneself," to become recognized by one's own accomplishments, to gain status and, hopefully, prestige. Inherently, there's nothing wrong with all of that. It's part of becoming your own person—part of establishing your place in the world. Unfortunately for most salespeople, their job becomes more than *part* of their identity. It becomes *all* of their identity, and very few know it has happened. In the pursuit of the almighty dollar and sales immortality, many salespeople begin selling their souls.

It only takes a few years for some—for others, maybe a decade or two—but eventually, instead of finding themselves in their work, many salespeople begin to lose themselves. I'm not talking about a midlife crisis here. This is a different sort of crisis that spans the spectrum of age, status, and sales industry.

A man I've known for almost a decade lives a story that's far too common. We'll call him Sam.

He once had a good family for whom he wanted to provide well and some close friends who were helping him along the way. He was a good man with a lot of ambition. He worked hard at his trade and told me he wanted to become the top sales professional in his industry. After a few years, he started making some decent money, and it began to look as if his dream might become a reality. Then one day I found out he had made it—he was listed in the top 1 percent of his industry nationwide. He was probably making a seven-figure income. It was quite an accomplishment.

But I began to hear conflicting reports. When I probed deeper into the situation, I discovered that while he had managed to become successful by financial standards, he was a relational nightmare.

I spoke with some of his former coworkers, and all had the same story. Sam was a workaholic who had sold his soul to sales and, in the process, sold out all his friends and family. In his climb to so-called success, he'd become a backstabber, a crook, a man with no integrity—anything to make himself more money. He won his millions by befriending successful people, then betraying them when the time was right. I also discovered that his happy marriage ended in an ugly divorce at his own negligent hand, and most of the people he once called friends were no longer speaking to him.

Today, he still attends my events because he sees them as networking opportunities to further his business. When I see him walking around, he's well put together and all smiles. But on the inside I know he's in shambles. If he was ever down and out, I don't know if he'd have anyone to help him. I can only hope that, as he sits in the audience for the fortieth time, he begins to hear what we're trying to teach.

WORK SHAPES YOUR IDENTITY . . . FOR BETTER OR WORSE

It was Winston Churchill who said that at first we choose and shape our life's work, and then it shapes us. He meant that in a good way, as if to say, "You choose a line of work, and then that work helps you become a better you." It's an encouraging statement with that perspective. Unfortunately, a widespread inclination toward longer hours in sales makes Churchill's statement sound more like a prophetic warning—as if he was saying, "You choose a line of work to become a better you, but then that work changes who you are, oftentimes for the worse."

Most Americans during Churchill's era assumed that a person's work shaped him in positive ways. Although it wasn't yet the American labor movement's slogan, "eight hours for work; eight hours for rest; eight hours for what we will" was mostly a reality. Today the notion is just a tease. In fact, today you are compelled to ask of a sales job, is it shaping you positively or negatively?

It is true that work can mold us in good ways. As salespeople we can learn to better relate to people. We can learn to serve. We can learn to value teamwork and perseverance and communication. But as author Al Gini points out, work does much more than that, and often leads us into a trap.

> Work is at the center of our lives and influences who we are and all that we do . . . work is not just about earning a livelihood. It is not just about getting paid, about gainful employment. Nor is it only about the use of one's mind and body to accomplish a specific task or project. Work is also one of the most significant contributing factors to one's inner life and development.[2]

For most of us, work occupies the majority of our time and energy, and that, says Gini, is why our job "not only provides us with an income, it literally names us, identifies us, to both ourselves and others." We see this truth in our tendency to ask people we've just met, "So, what do you do for a living?" or, "What kind of work do you do?" We ask such questions because, like it or not, our identities are tied up in what we do for a living. How tied up? That depends on one thing. You guessed it: time.

TIME DEFINES YOUR IDENTITY

There's nothing wrong with work shaping *some* of your identity. To an extent, that's how it should be. It's great to be known as a hard worker and a successful salesperson. It's healthy and fair to be known for your career accomplishments and, to an extent, the position you hold. In fact, I can think of several people in history who are remembered for the work to which they dedicated themselves. But what if that is all we are known for? Is that what we really want? Isn't the work of a person tainted if we learn he abandoned family or disregarded friends or lived a double life of insincerity or ultimate regret in order to carry out his work?

The more time you spend working, the more your identity is tied up in your work.

"You can't smell the flowers when you're working twelve hours," sang Charlie King.[3] He was right. It's true that you can accomplish much if you give all of your time to something. But at what cost? Has any salesperson lived such a lopsided life and not regretted it in the end? Howard Hughes was arguably the savviest salesman of his time—the first American billionaire, with two presidents in his hip pocket and a stockpile of cash and comforts to last ten lifetimes. If anyone had reason to be proud, it was him, right? Apparently not. Hughes died alone in his penthouse with inches-long fingernails and needle marks peppering his arms. There was something more to that demise than a drug addiction.

Our own experience cannot lie. While work gives us much to be rightly proud of, we want to be identified by more than a job. It's a paradox of sorts. On one hand we esteem work; we hold it in high regard because of what it offers to us: a title, a position, a purpose. On the other hand, we would rather work less if we could. Why do you think people are so drawn to online trading and the Lottery and Las Vegas? Because we want to work *more*? Why did you pick a job in sales? Was it for the lack of stability and long hours? You see where I'm going with this.

Oh, you could probably find some statistics that show that a small percentage of salespeople are completely fulfilled by their jobs—but aren't they the minority? Work for most of us seems, well, like work. A necessity yes. Enjoyable—it can be. But the embodiment of who we are? Not quite.

If we can find purpose and meaning in our jobs, that's wonderful. And you absolutely can, but it's not by devoting all your time to it. It's by allowing work to promote something deeper—something more freeing and exciting and enduring. We've sought this out in the past few decades by working more, but it doesn't seem to be working as we thought. Depression is now the most expensive of all medical costs—70 percent higher than anything else—and stress is next in line.[4]

Besides, let's put statistics and arguments aside. Now—what does *your heart* tell you? Don't you desire more for yourself than more money and greater sales success?

LIVE TO WORK OR WORK TO LIVE?

Author Joe Robinson tells the story of a salesperson named Dana who was struggling with this identity paradox. According to Robinson, Dana is a single dad torn between his instincts as a 'go-to-the-wall' American to do whatever it takes to get his job done and his need to find time for his daughter and life." As a sales rep for Frito-Lay, Dana found himself trapped in the necessity of sixty-plus-hour workweeks.

Robinson cites the sales rep's inner turmoil: "There's nobody to take up the slack if there's a family issue that comes up, or if you get sick. You can't wake up in the morning and not feel good. Your work will just pile up . . . everyone wants more time from me . . . I know I'll never make it at this pace to retirement. Maybe the answer is to have a simpler lifestyle, to live out of a tent.[5]

Maybe you can relate.

Because many salespeople today give longer and longer hours to selling, they commonly end up with identities characterized solely by their work, although that's not really what we want.

In her insightful book *Married to the Job*, psychotherapist Ilene Philipson shares the following story of one saleswoman who illustrates the extreme of what we're talking about:

When Ingrid entered my office I was struck by this very attractive woman's faultless appearance. She wore an expensive tailored suit; her hair was a perfect brown bob; nothing was creased, askew, or less than understated elegance. As Ingrid spoke she revealed herself to be an extremely intelligent, articulate, thirty-nine-year-old woman, who, it seemed, had annexed her very being to the workplace . . .

Throughout her teens and early twenties she felt comfortable both being productive and having fun . . . She feels her life began to change when she entered an MBA program at one of the nation's leading business schools. The competition was intense, and the requirements of studying and working diminished the time and energy she had for her social life. Upon receiving her master's degree, she was hired by one of the largest, well-established Silicon Valley corporations. Ingrid worked there for four years, steadily moving up the corporate ladder, working long hours and thinking of little else besides her responsibilities, her interactions, her standing at work . . .

[Then] Ingrid was lured away from her job by a start-up company that I will call E-Stream . . .

Ingrid worked 110 hours a week. She describes sleeping on the conference-room floor for four hours in her clothes each night, then freshening up in the bathroom . . . She lost weight, never talked to friends or family, and one day found her tropical fish dead because she had neglected to feed them . . . She came to therapy at thirty-nine because she feels her devotion to work has "interfered with my outside life."

To understand the enormity of this statement one must know that Ingrid has no social contact outside work, and no one she can point to as a friend. She has not had sex in eleven years. She typically spends Christmas or New Year's at work, where, she states, "there's always something going on."[6]

The reality is that salespeople like Ingrid who work sixty-, seventy-, and eighty-plus-hour weeks *don't have time* to be identified by anything else. They spend very little time at home, so they are not identified by their family roles. They have little time to consistently pursue hobbies or interests, so they are not known for what else they might enjoy outside of work. They have little time for friends, so they are not known by their relationships or social graces. In fact, most hardworking salespeople spend any downtime they might possess trying to recuperate from the stress and strain of their schedules. To paraphrase Gini in *The Importance of Being Lazy:*

Unfortunately, for too many of us our various forms of recreation and play are really about rehabilitation, recuperation and recovery rather than rapture and the possibility of the rediscovery of self. This is because, for many of us, our play or diversions are really only momentary distractions from the usual pace of life. They are designed to overcome fatigue, numb awareness, or appease a particular appetite so that we can go back to the job to endure and earn more.[7]

Ultimately, when your time is monopolized by your *work*—and/or recovering from work—the only thing that forms your identity is *work*. You are known to yourself and to others solely by what you sell, how you sell, and how well you sell. You become lost in your job. It's an unenviable place that many sales companies are obliging of late.

It wasn't long ago that having a refrigerator at work was a big deal. Common today are full kitchens with every amenity, coed gyms, bathrooms complete with showers and lockers, child care, lounges with leather couches and big-screen TVs, and even corporate cafés so we don't have to leave the office to get a caffeine fix.

Workplaces have become increasingly domesticated. Philipson notes that *Fortune* magazine revealed that "46 of the 100 Best Companies [to work for] offer take-home meals to liberate people from having to cook dinner. Twenty-six of the 100 offer personal concierge services, allowing employees to outsource the time consuming details of buying flowers and birthday presents, planning bar mitzvahs, or, in the case of one Chicago suitor, organizing an engagement dinner."[8] She makes her point with the words of one employee interviewed by sociologist Arlie Hochschild, who explains, "In America, we don't have family coat of arms anymore, but we have the company logo."[9] In fact, work has permeated so much of our identity in American culture that we consistently work more hours per year than any other country—leapfrogging the notorious workhorse Japan in 2000 by thirty-seven hours a year.[10]

> *Ultimately, when your time is monopolized by your work—and/or recovering from work—the only thing that forms your identity is work.*

With so much time dedicated to selling, "When," asks Gini, "will there be time to be human? . . . As Benjamin Kline Hunnicutt so aptly put it, 'Having to go so fast to keep up, we miss stuff—our existence is truncated. Some things simply cannot be done going full speed: love, sex, conversation, food, family, friends, nature. In a whirl, we are less capable of appreciation, enjoyment, sustained concentration, sorrow, memory.'"[11]

TIME TO SUCCEED

While working out this morning, I noticed an ad on television; the sound was muted, and I saw only two captions during the thirty-second spot, but they made the point. The first caption asked,

Why do we work?

The second,

Why are you working?

The problem with an identity solely founded in work is fairly obvious if you are honest about the things you desire. Sure, we desire sales success; you wouldn't be reading this book if that wasn't the case. We also desire the boost of self-esteem and the shaping of character that come from having worked hard for success. But we desire so much more, don't we? You are reading this book to improve your selling productivity, right? But why *else* are you reading this book? Why *else* are you tired of being swamped at work? Why *else* are you working?

Now we're getting somewhere.

If you and I were having a lazy lunch on a Sunday afternoon and I asked you to define success, what would you say? Think about it, really. How would you define success *for you*?

I imagine that at first you might mention things related to work. Becoming the top salesperson in your office, or something like that. You'd probably mention something about how your success is related to the level of satisfaction you give your customers and the value you add to their lives. Maybe you'd talk about the quality of your product or service in relation to your industry's standards. All noble things, for sure. But the more you thought about it, the sooner you would begin to mention things that aren't related to work at all. If you are married, you'd probably relate success to the contentment and satisfaction you receive from your home life. You would likely begin to dream a little and talk about how you want your children to be great people. You might talk about spending time with good friends and helping them realize their dreams. Eventually you would bring up hobbies that you love and want to pursue. Writing a book. Seeing the world. Starting a charity foundation. Raising horses and working a ranch. Building a mountain home. Learning to play an instrument or fly or paint or take beautiful pictures or snow ski or . . . *you* fill in the blank. Take a moment to give your definition of success here:

_____

_____

_____

_____

Isn't life about more than work, after all? In the end, if your only identity was work-related, wouldn't you be disappointed? If others only remembered you as a successful salesperson, wouldn't they be missing the whole picture?

MISTAKEN IDENTITY

The trouble with an unbalanced identity is that it is hard to detect if you aren't looking for it. However, I've met few hard-working salespeople who, when faced with the reality of regret, didn't readily admit they were already garnering some of the negative consequences:

- ◆ Guilt
- ◆ Restlessness
- ◆ A growing frustration
- ◆ An urge to justify their schedules
- ◆ Fear of regret
- ◆ Confusion
- ◆ Complexity
- ◆ Anxiety
- ◆ Fatigue

The signs reveal that while you may not have completely lost yourself, an all-work identity doesn't feel right. And it was never meant to. Author Joe Robinson reminds us of a time when it was easier to identify with things just as important as work:

Only a couple of decades ago a vacation was considered a well-deserved break in the action, a time for the family to hit the Great American Highway in search of campgrounds, Tasty Freezes, and the greatest prize of all, the motel swimming pool. The summer vacation was a hallowed ritual in my family. Every year my dad would pile us into the station wagon, pick a direction, and we'd be hugging the asphalt of Southern California to eternity. No air-conditioning, just a windblown horizon of big skies, scenic outlooks, and busted radiators. Going without a vacation would have been unthinkable in the 1960s.

But something happened. American salespeople began handing the keys of their identity over to their careers. We began devaluing life in order to earn a better living. Says Robinson:

> Beginning in the early 1980s something began to snap in the national R&R psyche . . . The much-ballyhooed four-day week turned into a hallucination. The ability to break free of the office and savor down-time disappeared, swallowed up by a vortex of spiraling work hours and a fixation on productivity that has devalued all that is not attached to a task or a paycheck . . . We have euphemized a workplace without end.
>
> But no matter what you call it, it's a habit people would like to break.[12]

I hope he's right, because if we are to ever recapture our true identity, something of the status quo has to change.

Let's work with less stress, and sell more in less time, and get out of this swamp we're in—but first let's make sense of your work.

TRAPPED?

Certainly there are many real factors that seem to compel us to give more and more time to our jobs, including corporate downsizing, advances in technology, greater competition, higher cost of living, and the potential for bigger financial gains, to name the most popular. But in an unfortunate twist of fate, what begins as an honest attempt to stabilize our futures—and quite possibly realize them sooner—ultimately changes our present lives into something that will never produce the futures we desire.

Not only does an identity wrapped up in work sap your identity, it keeps you from realizing your dreams.

Not only does an identity wrapped up in work sap your identity, it keeps you from realizing your dreams. In essence, it changes who you are now and who you will become in the future. Take a look at the trade-offs many salespeople (unthinkingly) make in order to maintain their mistaken identities.

This ... for ...	That?
Multilateral satisfaction	Unilateral success
Family fitness	Financial potential
Childhood dreams	Corporate vision
Needs	Wants
Pastimes	Products
Personal identity	Public position

Not many would make the trade-offs if they really considered the implications. But then again, we're talking about a trap, aren't we?

I realize that many salespeople—quite possibly you—don't want their lives to be defined by work alone, but most feel their options are very limited. If they work less, they will produce less. They will make less money. Things that need to get done, won't. The competition will eventually surpass them, leaving them, God forbid, out of a job. For most salespeople, the idea of downshifting the amount of hours they dedicate to work sounds like a slow-but-sure death sentence. "It doesn't seem possible to get everything done in less time" is the most common response I hear. But you're still reading, aren't you? Obviously, you hope that it *is* possible.

Be encouraged, because you're right—it is.

Rethinking Your Time and Recapturing Your True Identity

As I study the salespeople that are not repeatedly swamped by their work, I can trace in almost every case a point of epiphany where each gained a new perspective on time. As I prodded further, I found that each of them came to six common conclusions about time before they were able to make a change in how they used their time. I share these with you now because they are the foundation of everything else we will discuss:

1. Life will never settle down until I choose to settle it down.
2. Working is not living.
3. Time is life first, then money.
4. More work usually means less life; less work, more productivity and efficiency, usually means more life.
5. How I use my time deeply impacts my self-esteem, my identity, and my fulfillment.
6. I cannot control time, but I can control how I use and respond to time.

The implications of these truths will become more evident in the chapters to come. For now, there are a couple of things you need to do in order to begin to reclaim your identity and set the stage for regaining control in your days.

First and foremost, you must understand what is currently defining your identity. Who *you are* and *who you are becoming* is foundationally a function of how you are using your waking hours. Most salespeople overlook this in their pursuit of success and become something they never intended to be. This principle, however, is fairly simple to understand: what you invest your time in defines who you are. There is no way around this. If you devote sixty, seventy, eighty hours a week to anything, that thing will certainly play a big role in characterizing you—often the *biggest* role.

What you invest your time in defines who you are.

Here's a little exercise to help you distinguish what is currently responsible for defining your identity.

Take a moment and look over the following list of categories:

◆ Family

◆ Friends (this includes time on the phone)

◆ Church

◆ Volunteer work

◆ Job

◆ Leisure (this includes time *by yourself* reading, watching TV or movies, napping during the day, or simply reflecting on your life in a journal or in prayer)

◆ Hobbies

◆ Shopping (in stores or on the Internet)

◆ Exercising

◆ Managing finances/Investing

◆ Planning for the future

◆ Household duties (cleaning, landscaping, laundry, etc.—this does not count as family time or leisure or exercise)

Second, consider how you've been investing your time over the last week—get out your calendar or day planner to remind yourself, if necessary. In the space below, jot down the top five categories from the above list to show how your waking hours were invested, ranking them from first to fifth based on the most to the least amount of time you invested in them. Remember, we're talking about *all* your time, not just your work hours. There's no need to overthink this. These categories should stick out to you quite obviously.

1.

2.

3.

4.

5.

Now, to the best of your knowledge, assign a *daily* quantity of time to the right of each category. This can be in either hours or minutes, or both. Some of them may be rather low, but don't cheat yourself here. Be gut-level honest, even if you don't like what it's telling you.

The purpose of this exercise is to shed some light on why you've been stuck in the Identity Trap. Not only that, it reveals to you what things are currently defining who you are. I'm certain you can probably see where we're headed—but be patient. The answers you need to redefine your identity can't be communicated in one chapter. It's a process that we'll complete over the course of this book.

What I want you to understand—in fact, what you *must* understand before we go any further—is that *the only thing that will get you out of the swamp you're in is changing what you spend time on.* In other words, while you *cannot* manage or tame or recapture time, you *can* manage, prevent, and change most of the events that fill it up.

Here's some news that's encouraging in an unexpected sort of way: 75 percent of what you spend your time on at work is probably a waste of time. I'm serious—it's unnecessary and can either be eliminated or tapered significantly without depleting your productivity. My own interviews of salespeople in the top industries, and the cumulative results of our event surveys, all indicate that most salespeople waste at least three-fourths of their day on things that don't directly affect their bottom line. While that realization is probably a frustrating one, it should also

> *The only thing that will get you out of the swamp you're in is changing what you spend time on.*

encourage you that there truly is room for improvement. If you're in the majority, there is *plenty* of room. You see, when you begin to clean up the wasteful activities that you spend time on at work, you may not be as swamped as you think. Furthermore, you will have a lot more time to spend on the things you are currently neglecting.

In order to recapture your true identity you must accomplish two things:

- ◆ *Determine how you are wasting your time.*
- ◆ *Determine how to spend more time on the things that produce the life you desire.*

Your true identity will be shaped, and your path to freedom will become clear as you accomplish these objectives.

I can't promise you it will be easy. There are other traps that stand in your way and steal your time. The names alone may sound familiar to you. But let's not get ahead of ourselves. In the next chapter I will introduce you to a very simple system that will help you avoid these traps so you can begin reaping the results you desire from your time, on and off the job. The Identity Trap is discussed first, because I've found that when salespeople understand the real implications of being swamped, they are much more motivated to make changes in how they work. I hope that is your feeling now.

But before you turn the page, I want you to do something for me.

Take a couple of deep breaths.

Relax.

Get comfortable, and do your best to focus on what we're discussing. This is not a book you want to hurry through. But I promise you, in the end it will be well worth your time.

Executive Summary

In quintessential America, working long hours has become the norm, even the expectation. The salesperson who puts in seventy, eighty, even a hundred hours a week and is met with professional success is praised. We revere the long-hour-laboring salesperson. But what is often overlooked are the effects long hours have on one's identity. Sure, work is good for us. It gives us a sense of purpose and a feeling of accomplishment. But there's a fine line between successful selling and selling your soul to sales.

How you invest your time determines who you are now and who you will become. That's why your sales job shapes your identity for better or worse. The more time you give to it, the more your identity is wrapped up in selling—and the less your identity is defined by your other values, such as being a spouse, a friend, a parent, or maybe a fitness enthusiast, a wonderful cook, or a world traveler. Too much time given to selling, and who you are becomes solely what you sell.

However, if given the choice, most want to be known by more than their sales position and product. And the only way to ensure that happens is to balance the time you give to work with the time you give to the other things that make you who you are. There are two steps you must take to make this change: (1) determine how to spend less time at work (without losing sales), and (2) determine how to spend more time on the other things you enjoy in life. Both of these are a function of pursuing your truest definition of success.

Chapter Three

The Organization Trap

Wasting Time Juggling Unnecessary Tasks

Society often demands more of a man's nature than he can give.

—Thorne Lee

What if we put in shorter hours and got the work done anyway?
Don't laugh. Some people are doing it.

—Amy Saltzman

It varied the older you got—but when you were young, there was always a prerequisite to having free time. Completing your chores, finishing your homework, cleaning your room. Something like that, right? Whatever it was, the gist of the message was that you couldn't do what you really wanted to do with your time—hang out with the neighbor kids, watch TV, roam the mall with your friends—until your work was done and things were in their places. It was a rule meant to teach you a sense of order. Work came first, and only after it was done came play.

Many salespeople still hold themselves to the same rule.

The problem is that in sales the work is *never* done. At the end of the day, there is always one more call to make, one more e-mail to send, one more contract to draw up, or one more report to finish. The sales world revolves around others whose wants and needs don't diminish when the clock hits 5:00 PM.

There is always more you can do. That heavy feeling is only compounded by the fact that most of our tasks fall into the ASAP category. As salespeople, we are flooded with to-dos every day, and trying to get organized often feels like struggling to stack rocks in the middle of a raging river.

THE RIVER OF RESPONSIBILITIES

The Klamath begins as a river should, with a tall waterfall cascading from the south edge of a lake set amid the pristine pine mountains of southern Oregon. From beneath the falls the river begins its southwestward descent toward the California border. It flows through the Topsy Reservoir and into northern California and Copco Lake and eventually through the Iron Gate Reservoir on its way to the Pacific. It is to this seventeen-mile stretch south of the Reservoir, known as the Upper Klamath, that white-water-rafting enthusiasts flock in late spring, when snowmelt and April showers swell the river beyond its borders and the heavy water tumbles at eighty-five feet per mile.

During mid-May the Upper Klamath is typically at its highest and most treacherous level. Its water rushes deep and wide over the volcanic canyon floor, forming some thirty mammoth rapids. Rocks that normally arch above the surface untouched are instead veiled by dashing white shrouds of current. Certain-shaped boulders force portions of the surface inside itself, creating sinkholes spread randomly along the river like mines in a field. If your raft crosses one just right, the downward suction can yank the entire boat under and keep it there for days. River guides tell you of tragedies so you don't forget what you're up against. The Upper Klamath is not a place for beginners. It is a stretch of river that commands respect, and one that has taken the lives of many careless rafters.

But for those who know how to guide their rafts along its relentless May current, the Upper Klamath is as exhilarating a ride as you'll ever experience.

It's much the same in the sales profession.

Some days your river of re-sponsibilities flows steadily and predictably. You can pace yourself and complete your tasks without difficulty. You can foresee the obstacles in your path that threaten to slow your productivity and easily maneuver around them. If mistakes are made, you can correct them with minimal loss of time. When the river is steady, it is possible to get to work at a decent hour and be home for dinner. But let's face it: such days are a rare exception.

On most days your river of responsibilities probably rages like a mid-May, flood-high current that threatens to drown you. The more tasks rain down, the more disorganized and out of control you become. Even if you see obstacles, you rarely have the time or the energy to avoid them. Furthermore, getting organized at this rapid pace is at best a daunting task, at worst, a lost cause.

It seems the bane of the salesperson's existence: a fast-running, often-raging current of responsibilities that rises like a river in spring. I understand this state of affairs, because I've been there too. I've put in the long hours and still felt as though it wasn't enough. I have felt overwhelmed by the amount of tasks that I had to accomplish in a day. In fact, this is a circumstance I have to continually work to avoid, as do most sales-people, because we usually aren't the most structured people.

You Have an Excuse . . . Sort of

When I ask any ten salespeople to tell me the one thing they struggle with the most, at least eight tell me they are disorganized and lack the time to catch up. As a result, they scramble to get work done every day, but often at the expense of great inefficiencies and gross errors. It's a trap of sorts, really. To get organized takes time. It takes thought-out decisions and purposeful actions. But what hardworking sales-person has time for that? Once you're in the middle of the river and the current is sweeping you along, stopping to get organized only compounds the problem.

To make matters worse, most salespeople are haphazard by nature.

It may relieve you to know that there are actually psychological reasons for your hectic work ethic. An excuse? Not really. But it's at least a viable explanation for how you got to where you are.

Most salespeople test out in the highly driven or highly relational personality categories according to the DISC model.[1] Not surprisingly, these two personality types have the most difficulty when it comes to

	Driven Salesperson	Interpersonal Salesperson
Basic Descriptors	Daring Direct Dominant Decisive	Inviting Inspiring Infectious Indomitable
Emotional Default	Anger	Optimism
Characteristics	Risk Takers Need to Lead Desire to Win	High Emotions Need to Interact Desire to Be Liked
Quick Indicators 1. Extrovert/Introvert 2. Task/People Oriented 3. Direct/Indirect	Extroverted Task Oriented Direct Communicators	Extroverted People Oriented Indirect Communicators
Value to the Team	Challenge Oriented Self-Motivators Forward Thinking	Highly Optimistic Team Players Motivational
Possible Limitations	Overstep Authority Impatient Argumentative	Over-Sell Impulsive Lack of Detail

achieving organization. Take a look at a snapshot of these two personality types to see if you fit into one or both categories.[2] Indicators are very high that you do.

The highly driven salesperson is a task-oriented, outgoing individual who thrives on getting things done. The problem is that this salesperson tends to be impatient and will move on to the next thing if a task is dragging on or not reaping an immediate and tangible reward. As a result, he is always changing priorities and thus overloading his plate. Once swamped, the driven salesperson succumbs to a multitasking strategy, which he sees as a challenge. Unfortunately, this pattern leads to a decrease in work quality and an increase in work time. Deep down, this angers the driven salesperson, but he keeps telling himself, "Hard work pays off in the end."

The highly relational salesperson is also outgoing, but instead of being task oriented, she is people oriented and thrives on influencing people by building relationships. The problem is that the highly relational salesperson tends to be impulsive and to overcommit. Furthermore, while this person excels through communication skills, she tends to overlook the details required for good follow-through. As a result, she is constantly shuffling priorities to satisfy customers, which monopolizes her time. She thus never gains a real sense of control of her days, but she tries to look on the bright side. It is the interpersonal salesperson who claims, "Being busy is a good problem."

Do you see yourself in one of these people? Maybe both? While this information might explain some of your tendencies and blunt some of the frustration you've been experiencing, it doesn't solve the problem. I wanted you to see this data because I believe it affirms our need as salespeople to take strong measures to get our days under control. Our tendency is to remain out of control and resign to working harder to counterbalance this problem, but there are more productive measures we can take. (*If you would like to learn more about your style of selling and understand your customers' buy-ing styles, visit the following Web sites: www.buildingchampons.com or www.PlatinumRule.com.)*

LESSONS FROM A RIVER GUIDE

Brent, my writing partner, spent two summers guiding the Upper Klamath River, and a couple of the lessons he learned provide us with some great insight for beginning to overcome our incessant flood of responsibilities. Don't worry about what actions to take yet. Just consider the truth of these two lessons, and allow them to construct a mental foundation for cleaning up your days. Then you will be primed to take the necessary steps to achieve a place of sanity and simplicity in your schedule.

1. *Acknowledge the power of the river.* One of the requirements of Brent's training was jumping into a Class III rapid with waves that crested at about six to eight feet. In case you don't know, the rapids in western states are generally classified from I to V, Class V being the most dangerous. A Class III is a rapid whose danger often lies in the sheer power and volume of the water. Large rocks do not usually pose a serious threat, but the mere pace and power of the Class III current can take your breath away if you're not careful—it can effortlessly flip a full ten-person raft upside down. It was into this type of rapid that Brent was required to hurl his body, inhaling big on the peaks of the waves and holding his breath when the current forced him under. He says it was a struggle just to keep his head above water. He also says that after the experience, he plainly understood how easily a big cur-rent can take a person's life.

Early on in a sales career, it might seem like a fun challenge to take on everything that comes your way. But the longer you sell, the sooner you realize that the pace of a sales career doesn't slow down involuntarily. The more responsibility you assume, the faster the river travels, and it can eventually drown you if you underestimate the force of its current. It can leave you struggling just to keep your head above water. You must first acknowledge the life-sapping power of your river of responsibilities if you are to ever muster the courage to overcome its unforgiving current.

2. *When the river is high and fast, you must scout what's ahead.* This often requires that you pull out of the current and determine the right path. On a steep section of the Upper Klamath looms one of its most daunting rapids. Large boulders on each bank force the path of the swift current through an opening barely big enough for one raft. Normally this funnel effect would make for a fun ride and require simple technique, but there is one very big problem: a canine-shaped boulder reverently named "Dragon's Tooth."

Only ten feet beyond the small funnel-like opening, a giant granite tooth shoots out of the white water, forcing the rafter to pick a side or be eaten alive. The tooth isn't cordial; it stands dead center of the rushing current's path, daring the guide to avoid it. It couldn't be more in the way. As a result, the powerful current rushes smack into the tooth's face. For a raft to follow suit is perilous. The water is too powerful, and the rock is too big. For this reason, the most seasoned guides paddle ashore to walk the banks of the river and scout the best route to take. This isn't a cowardly move; quite the contrary, it's what every wise guide knows to do to protect and preserve their own lives and the lives of those in their raft.

If you're swamped, you've probably come to a place where your "Dragon's Tooth" is in view. You know you have to do something, anything, or your condition is about to get worse—completely out of control. Maybe as a result of working so much, your family is slowly falling apart. Or maybe your long hours have caused you to put on weight, and you're worried about the damage the stress is doing to your body. Maybe you're just sick of working so much, and you are about to crack if something doesn't change. You probably want to get back to spending time on other things you love, or to at least have some choices with your time . . . but I bet you're not sure how to get there. Now is an ideal time to pull off this raging river we call a sales career, if only for a few moments, and survey the scene to determine how you can make it through in one piece. From the bank, things become a little clearer.

DAMMING YOUR WORKLOAD

When you get out of the chaotic current of your career long enough to give it an honest look, you realize there are only two ways to manage your raging river of responsibilities:

1. You can learn to guide yourself through the rapids and attempt to avoid the obstacles as best as you can, or . . .
2. You can build a dam.

Being an ambitious lot, salespeople typically go for the first option. The floodgates are opened when they take their first sales job, and for the rest of their careers they do their best to avoid drowning. Does that sound about right? It's not necessarily every day, but it certainly describes a lot of our days.

It's not entirely your fault if you chose to take on the mighty sales river. Most managers preach that "it doesn't matter how it gets done, just get it done," so it's likely that when you started selling, you were thrown into the river and forced to learn on the go. As a result, you probably developed methods of working and selling that weren't the most efficient, but that got you by—techniques that allowed you to keep your head above water. Now, whether you've been at it six months or twenty years, you probably still utilize some of those diligent-but-not-so-efficient strategies.

The problem, however, is that you can't manage the flow of the river very well when you're in the middle of it yourself. This is why so many salespeople struggle to maintain organization in their days. When the current is sweeping you along, all you can do is keep your head above water and avoid the rocks and trees. You can't change the current, because you're part of it.

The only way to slow the pace of your river is to build a dam. Only then can you temper its relentless flow. History teaches us that, with a dam, even the biggest rivers can be tamed.

In 1931, thousands of men and their families traveled to Black Canyon, Nevada, to control the mighty Colorado. Their efforts are a testimony to people's ability to construct significant projects in the midst of adverse conditions. The Hoover Dam was the result, and it was built during the Great Depression with the following items:

- ◆ 5,500,000 cubic yards of excavated material

    1,000,000 cubic yards of earth and rockfill

    45,000,000 pounds of reinforcement steel

    21,670,000 pounds of gates and valves

    88,000,000 pounds of plate steel and outlet pipes

    6,700,000 pounds, or 840 miles, of pipe and fittings

    18,000,000 pounds of structural steel

- ◆ 5,300,000 pounds of miscellaneous metal

The amount of concrete in the Hoover Dam and power plant—4.36 million cubic yards—would "construct a monument 100 feet square and 2 miles high; would rise higher than the Empire State Building if placed on an ordinary city block; or would pave a standard highway 16 feet wide, from San Francisco to New York City."[3]

Building a dam was no easy task then, and it won't be for you either. But once a dam is constructed, it can regulate even the fiercest rivers (the water pressure at the base of the Hoover is 45,000 pounds per square foot!).

THE BLUEPRINT OF YOUR DAM

Dams are constructed to regulate the flow of a body of water. Essentially, dams are boundaries that safeguard against an excess of water at any given time and maintain a predictable, manageable current. If your desire is to regulate the floodwaters of your frenzied work schedule, you, too, must construct a similar boundary.

I've said it for years: if you don't put boundaries on your business, you won't have balance in your life. In other words, *without* boundaries on your work responsibilities, you won't have time for life responsibilities or opportunities. On the other hand, *with* boundaries regulating your flow of work tasks, your time for life takes on new possibilities. Let's talk about how to begin constructing this dam to temper the crazy pace of work that you're currently caught in.

> *If you don't put boundaries on your business, you won't have balance in your life.*

First you must understand that, since you cannot manage time, the only way to organize your day is by managing your daily tasks. Task management—not time management—is the foundation of organization. If you can learn to harness the tasks that crowd your days, you will realize more freedom with your time. This is a critical point that I don't want to oversimplify, because it is so crucial. Let's put it this way: the only way to free yourself from the traps that steal your time is to manage the things that occupy your time: *tasks*.

With that said, let's begin with the basics of building your task boundaries. As a whole, I will refer to this as building your dam.

The construction of your dam consists of four phases. Each phase represents different boundaries—different levels of the dam—that you must construct in order to slow down the rapid pace with which tasks fill up your river of responsibilities. If you construct these phases in succession, in the end you will have raised up a dam the size of the Hoover that will allow you to regulate even the greatest flood of tasks—including the one you're faced with at work right now. The four phases are these:

1. Accumulation

2. Admission

3. Action

4. Assessment

PHASE 1: ACCUMULATION

This is the foundational phase of your dam. In this phase you must learn to block all *unnecessary* tasks before they require your attention and sap your time. In other words, the primary goal of the Accumulation Phase is to set up boundaries that will prohibit interruptions or distractions from entering your river. The construction of these boundaries is the key to overcoming the Organization Trap. We'll get back to this in a minute.

PHASE 2: ADMISSION

Once you've stopped unnecessary tasks from sapping your time, you must set up boundaries to help you prioritize and schedule the tasks that still require your attention. That's why this phase is called "Admission"—in it you will determine how to *admit* legitimate tasks into your schedule in the most efficient manner possible. It is in this phase that you will learn to decipher the difference between *necessary* tasks and *productive* tasks and then set up boundaries that will allow you to maximize your time each day for what is most productive. (This phase covers the Yes Trap.)

PHASE 3: ACTION

In this phase you begin to carry out the tasks that are either *necessary* or *productive*, based on your boundaries in the Admission Phase. In the Action Phase of construction, you will learn to increase your overall productivity. Upon completion of the Action Phase, you will have constructed your entire dam—but there will still be one last phase. (This phase covers the Control Trap.)

PHASE 4: ASSESSMENT

Once you get to this phase, you will already have a solid system of boundaries—a dam—in place that will provide you at least four hours a day to sell. However, you can still fall into habits that hinder the productive time you've created. The Assessment Phase helps you avoid those obstacles and teaches you how to remain focused on the tasks that are not only the most productive in your business but also the most productive in your life. (This phase covers the Technology Trap, the Commission Trap, the Quota Trap, the Failure Trap, and the Party Trap.)

COMMENCING CONSTRUCTION

As you can see, there's not much to the system. It doesn't need to be complicated. In fact, from here on out the keys to constructing your dam and regaining control of your days are found by overcoming the time traps we will discuss.

As we continue, you may find that you've constructed part of your dam already—and that's great. If that's the case, I encourage you to use those sections in the book as a review and a chance to evaluate the effectiveness of your boundaries. As for the remainder of the book—keep with it. This system is simple to apply and will change not only the face of your days but also the overall look of your life.

Remember that, in the end, the value of creating more time is gaining more life—so that's what we're ultimately after.

Now, if you're ready to pick up some tools and build this dam of yours, let's get going. We've no time to waste, literally.

DAMMING TASKS
BEFORE THEY DAMAGE YOU

The first two phases of construction—Accumulation and Admission—are the foundation of your dam and represent steps you will take to either eliminate or regulate tasks from entering your river of responsibilities. Placing boundaries in these two phases—before you take action—is the key to organization; no matter how out of control you are now.

For now let's focus on damming unnecessary tasks before they can get to you. This will immediately help you gain a sense of order in your days.

Phase 1: Accumulation

So often, salespeople add stress and extra work on themselves by taking a reactive approach to working—in essence, doing whatever falls on their plates. This is highly unorganized and allows unproductive interruptions to litter your river and monopolize your time. To begin cleaning up your chaotic work schedule, follow these five guidelines to construct boundaries that regulate or eliminate the most common *unnecessary* tasks that clutter your days. Applying these guidelines will erect the foundation for your dam.

1. ***Don't give your personal digits to customers.*** I'm talking about your cell phone number, your home phone number, and your personal e-mail address. This is a common mistake, and do you know why? Because people use them. If salespeople give me their personal digits and I can't reach them at work, I try to contact them with the other means they've provided. Why wouldn't I? They've given them to me. Don't you do the same thing? Yes, we are in a customer-service business, and you don't want to miss out on important calls, but if you don't begin to put boundaries on your customers' ability to get in

Don't give your personal digits to customers.

touch with you, you're never going to get out of the swamp. A nice salesperson gave me a business card the other day that listed seven ways to get in touch with her. Why give customers so many options? Make it simple for them and sane for you. Here's what I tell salespeople at my events: give prospects and customers only one e-mail address and one phone number. I know it's tempting and easy to justify giving out more contact information, but don't. Ask yourself this: Would I rather be known as easily accessible or worth waiting for?

2. ***Don't give your work digits to friends.*** If they already have them, ask your friends to e-mail and/or call you on your personal lines

instead. If the problem persists, ask your boss if you can change your digits (e-mail and/or phone number) and explain that you are working toward increasing your productivity. Okay, I know you're thinking that this is a bit extreme, but how many ways do our friends need to get hold of us? If you have a personal cell phone, a private e-mail address, and a home number (most of us do), your friends already have three ways to get in touch with you and leave messages. That's more than enough. You have to realize that if there is an emergency (the excuse that many people use for doling out their work digits to friends), people can get in touch with you, no matter where you are. The idea is to avoid all nonemergency calls and e-mails from friends, which make up about 99.9 percent of the total.

3. *Turn off the instant message and e-mail alert functions on your work computer.* I shouldn't need to tell you to do this, but I've found that many salespeople keep one or both of these functions on while at work. If you are checking and retrieving your messages at specific times (we'll discuss this in the next chapter), you don't need to know if you have messages until those times. The last thing you need is one-liners and alerts popping up on your screen all day. They are too tempting and will whittle away your time quicker than you realize.

4. *Don't answer the phone unless it is someone you are expecting.* How many of your unexpected calls end up leading to sales? Very few, if you're like most salespeople. Therefore, you don't need to be answering the phone every time it rings. In fact, unless you are a retail salesperson whose business comes via phone, or you are expecting a call, you shouldn't even have the ringer on. You may even want to cover the red Message Waiting light with black tape. If your cell phone beeps or vibrates when you have a message waiting, turn off that function too. I know that may seem a bit antisocial of

you—especially if you're in a big office with lots of coworkers—but the fact is that if there isn't a prospect or customer on the other end, you don't need to be on the phone. And as far as your coworkers go—they'll find a way to get in touch with you if it's important.

5. *Don't check your personal e-mail during work hours.* This is probably discussed in your five-hundred-page company policy manual, but let's stop pretending. Very few people abide by that rule, and it adds to your work hours—sometimes several hours a week. Not only that, it adds tasks to your river of responsibilities, like e-mailing so-and-so with a phone number, or calling so-and-so with directions, or checking out a Web site, or answering a question that can be answered later. Again, your friends will generally support you when they understand that you are taking steps to achieve order in your work time so you will reap more free time in return. If you don't have a laptop or a home computer, this can be a difficult step to implement. There are two ways to remedy this: (1) talk to your manager and request a laptop to replace your desktop. Most companies lease their computers, so this may be more feasible than you think. Or (2) invest in a home computer. There are many desktops that can be purchased for under $1,000 or that you can pay off with monthly payments. (For tax purposes this can also be considered a nonreimbursed business expense.) If you can't afford this route, you can lease a laptop for next to nothing and use it at home to catch up with friends. Whichever way you decide to go, your increased productivity at work will offset the expense in no time.

WORK WITHOUT INTERRUPTIONS

Permit me to skip over all the obvious escapism tasks that salespeople get into, like surfing the Web and playing computer games and telling jokes with coworkers in the kitchen. These are clearly a waste of time, and you need to eliminate such tasks if you desire to clean up your time. Those mentioned in the previous section represent the most pervasive, but often overlooked, time sappers in the sales industry. There are others, of course: needless meetings; incessantly straightening up your work area; reading the paper in the bathroom (let's be honest, guys); constantly "freshening up" in the ladies' room (you're not off the hook either, ladies); snacking every hour; fixing the broken copier; checking stocks, sports scores, or shopping malls online . . . Have I made my point? There are seemingly endless *unnecessary* tasks that can saturate our days. As trite as they may seem, you'll be surprised at how much time is freed up by simply constructing boundaries that keep such tasks from ever entering your river of responsibilities—beginning with the five most prevalent.

If in modest estimation you currently spend the following amounts of time each day on the five most pervasive tasks, take a look at how much time you will free up over the course of a year if you are able to block them:[4]

Task	Time Wasted	Time Freed
Personal e-mails to work address	30 mins/day	115 hours/year
Personal calls to work phone(s)	30 mins/day	115 hours/year
Answering every call	60 mins/day	230 hours/year
Customer calls to personal digits	60 mins/day	230 hours/year
Instant messages & e-mail alerts	15 mins/day	57.5 hours/year
Total time freed up	3 hours/day	747.5 hours/year

If you're thinking these are high estimates, I challenge you to tally your time for three weeks. I think you'll find that the figures are not far off. Can you imagine how much more you could accomplish with 747.5 more hours a year? That's almost nineteen more weeks!

Ahhh, the possibilities.

But of course, freeing up your time is more than keeping unnecessary tasks from interrupting you. As you know, many tasks cannot simply be eliminated. Organization, then, is also regulating the scheduling of tasks that you must carry out, but that may or may not be highly productive. This is the next task-management phase and the subject of our next chapter.

Executive Summary

Most days, getting organized amid the chaos of selling feels like trying to keep your head above water in a fast and high river. Often, your river of responsibilities rages like a mid-May, flood-high current that threatens to drown you. The more tasks rain down, the more disorganized and out of control you become. Even if you see obstacles, you rarely have the time or energy to avoid them. Furthermore, staying in control at this rapid pace is at best a daunting task, at worst, a lost cause. And to make matters worse, salespeople are characteristically unorganized.

The majority of selling disarray, however, is not the result of character flaws, too much work, or too little time. It is primarily the result of investing your time in meaningless tasks. Therefore, the first step to cleaning up your days is creating boundaries that keep *unnecessary* tasks from sapping your time:

1. Never give your personal digits to customers.
2. Don't give your work digits to friends.
3. Turn off the instant message and e-mail alert functions on your computer.
4. Don't answer the phone unless you are expecting a call.
5. Avoid checking your personal e-mail during work hours.

Metaphorically speaking, these five boundaries represent the initial construction of a dam that will eventually slow the current of your river of responsibilities. This initial phase is referred to as damming your accumulation of tasks.

Chapter Four

The Yes Trap
Wasting Time Saying Yes

I can't say no.

—RODGERS AND HAMMERSTEIN,
SONG FROM OKLAHOMA

It has been estimated that a typical salesperson has 170 interactions every day.[1] If you break this estimation down based on a 50-hour workweek, the numbers are telling: 170 interactions per day multiplied by 5 workdays per week equals 850 interactions. Divide these 850 weekly interactions by 50 work hours a week, and you find that you have about 17 interactions every hour. Or, in other words, you have about 3 minutes to focus on any one thing without interruption. Even if you work 80 hours a week to catch up, you will still only have about 5 minutes to focus on one task without interruption. Not only is this rarely enough time to get anything done *right*; it's rarely enough time to get anything done, *period*.

The problem is simple: most salespeople take on too many responsibilities, and this not only increases their time on the job, it increases their propensity for stress and oversights. One busy salesperson I read about purchased tickets to the World Series for some high-profile clients. She told the broker from whom she purchased the tickets that she wanted to attend a game on either Tuesday or Wednesday night, but preferably Wednesday. Imagine her shock when she met up with her clients at the gate on Wednesday night and was turned away because she held tickets for the night before. In a flurry, she had forgotten to look at the date.[2]

The busyness dilemma shows up in many ways: tardiness, forgetfulness, inconsistency, inefficiency, frustration, stress . . . there are many more, but busyness is rooted in only one thing: salespeople say yes too often. As a result, they end up starting more tasks than they finish every day, and the tasks they do complete are often riddled with errors or inconsistencies. This is only the beginning of woes, as you know, for when tasks are amiss, more time must be taken to revise or redo them. Furthermore, if tasks are begun and not completed one day, they spill onto the next day, compounding the workload and flooding your river of responsibilities until you are forced to either put in marathon days to "catch up," or concede to a whirling, flailing pace every day. And we all know that catching up is somewhat mythical, somewhat unattainable. It is being done by the superheroes of the sales world, who, legend has it, move so fast their movements are invisible to the naked eye. But is anyone *normal* catching up? Studies suggest that we aren't.

> *Busyness is rooted in only one thing: salespeople say yes too often.*

A typical day in the life of Super Salesman

Monday 9:01 AM   Monday 9:02 AM   Monday 9:03 AM

THE NEW "YES" ECONOMY

According to a 2001 phone survey of working American families conducted by the *Families and Work Institute*, the following conclusions were made:

◆ 55 percent are overwhelmed by how much work they have to accomplish.

◆ 45 percent feel they have to carry out too many jobs at once and multitask too often in order to keep up.

◆ 59 percent admit they are unable to reflect on and perfect the work they are doing.

◆ 90 percent strongly agree that they work "too fast" and "too hard" and they "never have enough time to get a job done properly."

We have become a laboring nation of yes-men and yes-women for whom no task is too much to ask and every task is commenced "Right away, sir" with a "Consider it done, ma'am" attitude. And salespeople are the leaders in this movement.

In sales it's easy to fall into the Yes Trap. Serving customers means granting requests, becoming, some might say, a genie-in-a-bottle of sorts. It means taking on tasks in order to gain rapport and close sales. It necessitates a can-do attitude. It takes a big investment of time. It requires you to become what Joan Williams, a law professor at American University, calls the "ideal worker." In *Work to Live,* Joe Robinson summarizes what this person looks like:

The ideal worker is someone who enters the full-time, now overtime, workforce in early adulthood, and, if he or she can, lifts their head forty years later.

However, there are problems to this label; Robinson explains one of them:

Ideal workers are hostages to their jobs, which makes them nonparents . . . The ideal worker role is a time bomb that blows up marriages, and kids are the collateral damage. The divorce rate is higher in overwork industries . . . In the end, the kids and all of us pay, says Williams, because 40 percent of divorced women wind up in poverty, and the children along with them, since most will live with the mother.[4]

Robinson calls this current working condition a "world where parents can't make a living and be a parent at the same time." It's tragic. But even if you're not a parent, the effects are extensive.

According to the National Sleep Foundation, 63 percent of American adults don't get the recommended eight and a half hours of sleep necessary for good health, safety, and optimum performance; nearly one-third report sleeping less than seven hours each weeknight. The study discovered a direct correlation between loss of sleep and the number of hours worked, indicating the need for Americans to find a way to scale back their hours on the job or suffer the consequences.

Most salespeople can admit to not getting as much sleep as they should. Unfortunately, most salespeople fail to make any headway on scaling back their workloads to accomplish this end, and therefore continue laboring in a constant state of stress and fatigue. It's not for lack of wanting, however.

Another NSF poll found that most workers indicate they are concerned about the impact of sleepiness and fatigue on a person's job performance. The poll found widespread support for limiting work hours for many professions that affect personal safety. Specifically, the poll found that:

◆ 70 percent believe the maximum number of hours worked each day by a doctor should be ten or less.

◆ 86 percent agreed that a pilot should be allowed to take a nap to overcome drowsiness while flying if another qualified pilot can take over; 63 percent said a pilot's maximum workday should be eight hours or less.

◆ Almost 50 percent supported limiting workdays of police officers, truck drivers, and nurses to a maximum of eight hours.[5]

These results indicate our acknowledgment of the need for change when one is spending too much time on the job. They also indicate our general agreement that long hours and sleep-deprived nights don't enhance job proficiency. At least that's what we think when it comes to doctors, nurses, truck drivers, police officers, and pilots. It's a different story when it comes to ourselves, isn't it? We feel trapped.

With an ever-rising flood of responsibilities, it seems impossible to scale back hours without squandering sales and shrinking success. But that's just how it *seems*. The truth is that if there are no limits to what you undertake, there are always regrettable consequences, and they're often worse than losing a few sales. At one of our recent events, Tim Sanders, the Chief Solutions Officer and Leadership Coach of Yahoo!, revealed that about eight million people suffer from what he calls NEDS. It stands for New Economy Depression Syndrome, and it's one adverse effect of the Yes Trap.

SCALING BACK WITHOUT LOSING SALES

There are only two ways to scale back your busy workload and free up more time: (1) sacrifice sales, or (2) say no more often. If you choose the first option, you are simply deciding that making less money is a fair trade-off for gaining more simplicity and sanity *on* the job and more time *off* the job. This is an admirable route, and if you choose it, I say more power to you. But it's not the most effective route—nor is it necessary.

In Chapter Two I told you it is likely that at least three-fourths of your time each day is spent on tasks that do not affect your bottom line. According to other studies, my statistics are modest.

In his latest book, Brian Tracy writes that in 1928, *Sales and Marketing Management* conducted a survey that revealed that the average American salesperson was selling only ninety minutes a day, or about 20 percent of the time at work. In 1988, thinking the increase in productivity training would surely have changed the efficiency of salespeople in America, the same magazine conducted a repeat survey. The results were the same: the average salesperson managed to grunt out ninety productive minutes a day. Nothing had changed in sixty years.[6]

More recently, in 2003, Proudfoot Consulting conducted a study of work behaviors and performance around the globe. For the first time since initiating the annual study, Proudfoot looked specifically at salesforce effectiveness.[7] They found that in every country surveyed (Australia, France, Germany, South Africa, Spain, the UK, and the U.S.), salespeople are bogged down in paperwork and customer-service issues and on average only spend 20 percent of their time actively selling and prospecting. Conversely, the study showed that the majority of salespeople spend about 43 percent of their time managing problems and administrative tasks and 30 percent of their time commuting to and from work and meetings with customers. The remaining 7 percent of their time is designated "downtime," during which nothing productive is accomplished. In other words, for nearly a century (or at least since we've been keeping track) salespeople around the world have spent about 80 percent of their time completing tasks that don't affect the bottom line. Take a look at the study's breakdown of time use by general category:

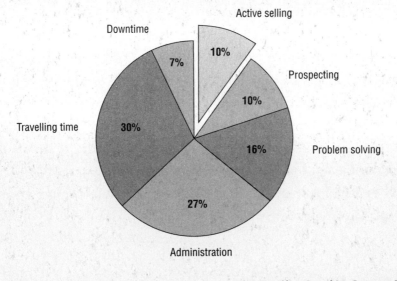

Now take a look at the breakdown of time use in the world's most prominent sales industries. Note the far left column, which indicates the average percentage of time spent "actively selling" in each industry.

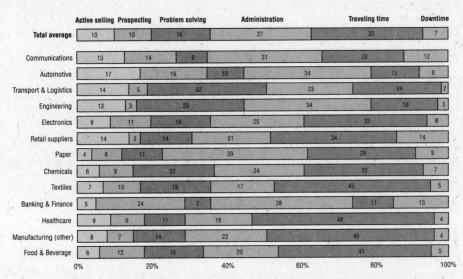

	Active selling	Prospecting	Problem solving	Administration	Traveling time	Downtime
Total average	10	10	16	27	30	7
Communications	13	14	8	31	22	12
Automotive	17	18	10	34	13	8
Transport & Logistics	14	5	32	23	24	2
Engineering	13	3	29	34	18	3
Electronics	9	11	16	25	33	6
Retail suppliers	14	3	14	21	34	14
Paper	4	8	11	39	29	9
Chemicals	6	9	22	24	32	7
Textiles	7	10	19	17	42	5
Banking & Finance	5	24	7	38	11	15
Healthcare	9	9	11	18	49	4
Manufacturing (other)	8	7	14	22	45	4
Food & Beverage	6	12	16	20	41	5

In the last chapter we discussed how we aimlessly take on tasks that monopolize our time. It's a trap we called the Organization Trap. To avoid it we must construct boundaries that regulate the accumulation of *unnecessary* tasks. This is essential to shelter your time and keep unproductive tasks from flooding your river.

In this chapter we're talking about something different. We're addressing a salesperson's inability to spend the majority of his or her time carrying out the most productive, bottom-line tasks. Clearly, it's a problem and has been for some time. I call it the Yes Trap, and it is rooted in a salesperson's inability to say no.

THE VALUE OF SAYING NO

If we take a detailed look at the general tasks that salespeople are saying yes to, we'll not only pinpoint the source of the problem, we'll discover a fresh solution you can use right away. Let's get started.

In the grouping of tasks that we carry out over any given day, there are three categories:

1. *unnecessary* tasks,

2. *necessary* tasks, and

3. *productive* tasks.

To make this easy to remember, think of the three categories as the three descending colors on a stoplight. We'll break these down more in a minute.

◆ *Unnecessary tasks* are *red* because they represent activities that prohibit your business from moving forward, and therefore waste your time. As discussed in Chapter Three, such tasks include e-mailing friends, answering unexpected phone calls, chatting with coworkers, instant messaging, making personal phone calls, Web surfing, and playing computer games. These are the tasks you need to stop.

◆ *Necessary tasks* are *yellow* because they represent the activities that have the potential to move your business in a positive direction but at a less productive pace than other activities. These activities are a good use of your time, but for strategic direction only. Such tasks include goal setting and planning, observation and evaluation, qualifying prospects, surveying customers, and dealing with paperwork necessary for the completion of a sale. This is your caution zone. These are tasks for which you need to regulate your time investment.

◆ *Productive tasks* are *green* because they represent the activities that most effectively move your business in a positive direction and are the best use of your time. They are often action(s) that reflect the discoveries you have made completing *necessary* tasks. The top two activities in this category are strategic prospecting and selling. There are no other tasks that add more to your bottom line. They are your "go" tasks. (As an aside, I would also include "knowledge gathering" in this category. I have a client who devotes ten hours of his free time per week gaining knowledge of the trends in his industry. Something similar can be accomplished outside of your work time by reading relevant publications and books on a regular basis. I recommend that at least every other publication or book you read be one that furthers your professional education.)

UNNECESSARY TASKS

NECESSARY TASKS

PRODUCTIVE TASKS

Let's discuss the details of each task category and determine how to construct boundaries that enable you to effectively regulate and schedule them.

UNNECESSARY TASKS

We dealt exclusively with the most pervasive unnecessary tasks in the last chapter, so I won't say much more here except to remind you that your boundaries in the Accumulation Phase are the foundation of your dam. You must maintain regulation of these time wasters through disciplined boundaries or you will never temper the current of your river of responsibilities. Initially, it should require no more than 5 percent of your work hours. Once you have cemented your boundaries and are comfortable with their effectiveness (this should take three weeks or less), you will no longer have to spend time on regulation in this category. Your dam will do the regulating for you.

That said, let's examine the other two categories and how you can set up boundaries to help you spend the majority of your work time on tasks that reap the greatest return in productivity and free time. Now we're on to the next phase of construction.

Phase 2: Admission

NECESSARY TASKS

The category of greatest struggle for salespeople is *necessary* tasks. This category includes everyday duties that offer value to your business and *can* free up your time if carried out properly. But if too much time is given to these tasks, you will end up wasting more time than you gain in return. Proceed with caution on *necessary tasks*; this is often where many good salespeople hit a ceiling on their productivity and thus cease to ever achieve greatness. One client found herself in this place when she sought out coaching. As it turned out, she'd been spending an average of 185 minutes a day on necessary-but-not-productive tasks. Finding a solution for decreasing the amount of time she was spending on these tasks became the focus of her coaching and the main reason her sales eventually tripled. That may be where you need to start as well.

The goal with necessary tasks is to spend high-quality time on them but not a high quantity of time. Let's highlight the main tasks in this category and briefly discuss the boundaries we must construct for them.

NECESSARY TASK #1: PAPERWORK

[TOTAL TIME INVESTMENT:
30 minutes every other hour, or 2 hours total per day]

This is a major time killer if boundaries are not in place, because it encompasses so many different tasks: filling out paperwork, faxing paperwork, copying paperwork, filing paperwork, etc. This is the most common bog-down area for salespeople.

The fact is we all have paper trails that are necessary for sales to happen. While this is never the best use of your time, there are a few ways you can spend less time on paperwork. Remember, the point of the Admission Phase is regulating *necessary* tasks in such a way that you can assess and act on them in a highly efficient manner.

The best way to accomplish this is to delegate your *necessary* paperwork to an assistant or team member. I will discuss this solution in the next chapter, as it requires more explanation than we will take time for here. For now, let's assume that an assistant or team is not yet an option for you. If that's the case, just keep applying the advice in this book and you *will* have a team of people helping you before long. The next most effective way to regulate time spent on paperwork is to block specific periods each day to deal only with these tasks—this way you're never interrupting your momentum on more productive tasks.

Time	Monday	Tuesday	Wednesday	Thursday	Friday
9:00	Tasks	Tasks	Tasks	Tasks	Tasks
9:30	*Paperwork*	*Paperwork*	*Paperwork*	*Paperwork*	*Paperwork*
10:00	Tasks	Tasks	Tasks	Tasks	Tasks
10:30	Tasks	Tasks	Tasks	Tasks	Tasks
11:00	Tasks	Tasks	Tasks	Tasks	Tasks
11:30	*Paperwork*	*Paperwork*	*Paperwork*	*Paperwork*	*Paperwork*
12:00	Tasks	Tasks	Tasks	Tasks	Tasks
12:30	Tasks	Tasks	Tasks	Tasks	Tasks
1:00	Tasks	Tasks	Tasks	Tasks	Tasks
1:30	*Paperwork*	*Paperwork*	*Paperwork*	*Paperwork*	*Paperwork*
2:00	Tasks	Tasks	Tasks	Tasks	Tasks
2:30	Tasks	Tasks	Tasks	Tasks	Tasks
3:00	Tasks	Tasks	Tasks	Tasks	Tasks
3:30	*Paperwork*	*Paperwork*	*Paperwork*	*Paperwork*	*Paperwork*
4:00	Tasks	Tasks	Tasks	Tasks	Tasks
4:30	Tasks	Tasks	Tasks	Tasks	Tasks
5:00					

Damming Your Paperwork

A good start is to block thirty minutes every other hour for paper-work. During this time—and only during this time—complete all the necessary paperwork that has accumulated over the previous hour and a half. With your time blocked accordingly, your weekly calendar would look like the chart on the next page. (for now we will just say the remainder of your work time is filled with "tasks")

Obviously, the less time you spend on paperwork, the more time you will free up to invest in productive tasks. Therefore, if you find that you don't need this much time each day, scale it back accordingly. I know salespeople who block the thirty minutes before lunch and the thirty minutes before they go home to do paperwork. These seem to be productive periods, as eating and leaving are great incentives to get the work done efficiently. Whatever you decide, make sure you block your paperwork time strategically so you won't have too much to complete. One way to ensure this doesn't happen is to set up a simple filing system that helps you separate what needs to be done immediately from what can wait. I use a system I call the Nifty Fifty and it can be set up like this:[8]

1. Pick up 50 hanging file folders

2. Divide them as follows:

3. Get 4 purple folders and label them Family, Fitness, Finances and Fun. (We won't discuss these here, but this is where all your ideas for these categories go. They are reviewed annually and go into the system described below.)

4. Label and number 31 green folders 1-31 for the days of the month

5. Label 12 yellow folders January through December

6. Label 2 blue folders with the current year and the following year followed by the word *Planning*

7. Label 1 red folder with the words *Improvements and Surveys.*

Here's how it works: When you have an upcoming paperwork task, you drop the necessary papers into the appropriate monthly folder according to when you need to complete it. On the last workday of the month, take out the next month's folder and sort its paperwork into your thirty-one daily folders. At the beginning of your blocked paperwork time each day, you will simply take out your appropriate daily folder and complete the paperwork filed there. You will be clearing the daily folders every day.

Once this system is underway, it flows very smoothly and makes it easy to stay on top of all your paperwork with minimal effort. (If you already have an assistant, have that person use the same filing system. You can then delegate to his or her folders and free up even more time. If you travel, take the folders for the days you will be gone, as well as the next month. If you have a vacation scheduled, don't file anything in the folders of the days you will be gone.)

NECESSARY TASK #2: PLANNING AND GOAL SETTING

[TOTAL TIME INVESTMENT:
8–24 hours per year; 15 minutes per week]

Spend one or two days planning once a year. Do this during a period when you will not be distracted by social plans or professional obligations. I do it between Christmas and New Year's—but if December is a long way off as you're reading this, then schedule it sooner.

During this time you will not only review your progress (or lack thereof) from the year that is about to end, but you will also set goals for the upcoming year for your business and life, and then determine specifically how you will accomplish these by recording specific daily, weekly, or monthly steps on paper. File these papers in one blue folder labeled with the current year and the word *Planning*, and review it every Monday morning before you begin working. If there are planning ideas for next year, keep that in next year's blue folder. You can do this at home or first thing in the office. Your Monday morning reviews should take no more than fifteen minutes, as your plans should be concise enough to be typed on one or two pages.

Mondays are not time for evaluation; they are just to position your personal and professional goals and values at the front of your mind as you begin your week. Here are a few: What new things do you need to learn? What clients need developing? How many prospecting calls need to be made? If you isolate yourself during your annual planning sessions and are careful to set realistic, value-centered goals, you will not have to spend time amending your plan throughout the year.

Necessary Task #3: Surveying Customers

[TOTAL TIME INVESTMENT:
5 minutes per sales transaction to conduct the survey]

Don't let this build up. Design or have designed a strategic survey that elicits the information you desire from your customers, and then ask for their feedback *before* you close the sale so that errors are quickly pinpointed and addressed. One of our favorite restaurants does this between the time you finish your entrée and before dessert and coffee are served.

AN EXAMPLE OF A SURVEY

Honest, critical feedback from you is the best way for us to stay in tune with your needs. Learning how we did after your order is fulfilled is valuable, but as a team we feel it is more important to understand how we are doing currently. If we are off, we want to correct our efforts now so that you have a good experience from now on. If we are on target, then we want to stay the course.

Please take just a few moments to answer 7 very brief questions using a scale of 1 (Poor)–5 (Best):

Have we done a good job of determining the right product solutions for your specific needs?

1   2   3   4   5

Have we returned your calls promptly?

1   2   3   4   5

Have we answered your questions to your satisfaction?

1   2   3   4   5

Have we kept you informed of the status of your order?

1   2   3   4   5

Have you found everyone on our team to be courteous and professional?

1   2   3   4   5

Are you pleased with the service our other departments are providing?

1   2   3   4   5

Can you make any suggestions on how we might serve you better?

_____

_____

Thank you for taking the time to help us. We appreciate you!

The last thing you want as a salesperson is a customer who pays you but feels bad about the service he received. That's why surveying is a *necessary* task. It's still not the most productive use of your time, so come up with a survey that is quick and to the point.

Once completed, keep your surveys in your red folder labeled with the current year and the words *Improvements and Surveys.* You want these saved and easily accessible because they provide great material for evaluating your progress during your observation and evaluation time. This is the next *necessary* task.

NECESSARY TASK #4:
OBSERVING AND EVALUATING

[TOTAL TIME INVESTMENT:

5 minutes every 60 minutes of your workdays for the first month; then,
when you're highly productive, spend 1 hour every month]

Early in my career, a salesman for a national insurance firm told me that he takes five minutes out of every sixty to evaluate his productivity. Spending forty minutes throughout the day making sure seven hours and twenty minutes goes well is a good idea. I recommend that you follow this model for your first month or until you feel that you are sustaining momentum. Then spend one hour on the last workday of every month observing and evaluating your progress against the goals you've recorded in your planning session. As I said above, you can also use your customer surveys as aids here—they will often help you identify some trends in your selling efforts and show you how to improve. Record your observations and necessary improvements on a sheet of paper and file them each month in your red folder labeled with the current year and the word *Improvements and Surveys.* If your improvements change your goals for the year, you can also move this paperwork to your *Planning* folder that you review every Monday morning.

Necessary Task #5: Communication

[TOTAL TIME INVESTMENT:
30 minutes every other hour or 2 hours total per day]

The final necessary task that steals so much of our selling time is communication. This includes two tasks: e-mails and phone calls with customers. When we discussed the Organization Trap in the previous chapter, I mentioned the need for you to set up boundaries to eliminate *unnecessary* communication: personal e-mails, personal phone calls, and giving customers your personal communication information. Now we are talking specifically about communication that is required for your business to succeed. Although these tasks are necessary in that you cannot close sales or maintain a high level of customer service without them, there are still boundaries that you must construct so they don't build up and breach your dam. These boundaries are created by strategically blocking periods of time to dedicate to the tasks.

Damming Your Communication

Most salespeople check voice mail and e-mail every time they return to their work spaces. If there are no messages, this is a sure waste of time. If there are messages that require action, this only adds to the stress of the day, especially when you are tempted to address the message or carry out the requested tasks immediately. Caught in this cycle, the average salesperson wastes approximately two hours a day treating every message as an emergency that requires immediate attention. One salesperson I coached spent twenty-five hours a week listening to and returning calls/e-mails before she built boundaries. After her boundaries were in place, her business boomed by nearly 200 percent because she had so much more time to be productive.

The fact is that most voice mail and e-mail messages can wait—

especially when you let others know of your explicit plans to return their communications. So instead of constantly checking for messages throughout the day and responding to them immediately and sporadically, determine two to four specific times that you will check and return calls or e-mails. Also, indicate with a voice mail greeting and an auto-response e-mail that you will be doing so.[9] This will reassure customers that you will call them back shortly and will aid in helping you not feel compelled to answer the phone.

Obviously, the less time you spend on communication, the better, but it's important that you don't ever appear rushed. Where e-mails are concerned, this is easier to avoid. When speaking with customers, it's okay to be to the point, but don't be so time conscious that you are impersonal or rude. Remember that your overarching goal in all communication is to foster trust with your customers. The best way to accomplish this without seeming rushed is to make a point to mention how much you value their time when you call.

Let customers know you want to be sensitive to their schedules and they will generally let you proceed. However, don't overlook that any time spent communicating with a customer is a chance to grow the relationship and must therefore be regulated with a soft boundary that allows you to, if necessary, spend more time than you've allotted if you believe it is furthering the relationship. I'm not talking about meaningless chatter. I'm talking about instances in your conversations when you have an opportunity to connect at a deeper level with customers. These moments are important to the longevity of your relationships, so be open to them.

My advice is to start modestly on your boundaries with necessary communication tasks and adjust as you get more comfortable. I usually advise salespeople to initially spend the first thirty minutes of every other hour checking messages and returning calls/e-mails. If we apply this to our schedule-in-progress, your weekly calendar would look like this:

Time	Monday	Tuesday	Wednesday	Thursday	Friday
9:00	Communication	Communication	Communication	Communication	Communication
9:30	Paperwork	Paperwork	Paperwork	Paperwork	Paperwork
10:00	Tasks	Tasks	Tasks	Tasks	Tasks
10:30	Tasks	Tasks	Tasks	Tasks	Tasks
11:00	Communication	Communication	Communication	Communication	Communication
11:30	Paperwork	Paperwork	Paperwork	Paperwork	Paperwork
12:00	Tasks	Tasks	Tasks	Tasks	Tasks
12:30	Tasks	Tasks	Tasks	Tasks	Tasks
1:00	Communication	Communication	Communication	Communication	Communication
1:30	Paperwork	Paperwork	Paperwork	Paperwork	Paperwork
2:00	Tasks	Tasks	Tasks	Tasks	Tasks
2:30	Tasks	Tasks	Tasks	Tasks	Tasks
3:00	Communication	Communication	Communication	Communication	Communication
3:30	Paperwork	Paperwork	Paperwork	Paperwork	Paperwork
4:00	Tasks	Tasks	Tasks	Tasks	Tasks
4:30	Tasks	Tasks	Tasks	Tasks	Tasks
5:00					

(I know some salespeople who retrieve voice mails one last time on their way home from the office, but I don't recommend this, as it creates unnecessary anxiety that decreases the quality of your evening time.)

You can obviously raise this boundary up or down based on how much of your business is conducted via phone and e-mail. But don't miss the point. By regulating your communication time, you increase the quantity of time that you can spend on your most productive tasks.

PRODUCTIVE TASKS

We will discuss how to increase your efficiency in prospecting and selling tasks in the coming chapters. For now, you simply need to understand that productive tasks (green-light tasks) don't need to be regulated. These are the tasks in which you want to invest as much time as possible. In other words, it is to these tasks that you always want to say yes. But that can only happen when you say no to unnecessary tasks, such as personal calls and e-mails, and place strategic regulations on necessary tasks, such as retrieving and returning messages.

If you keep to our schedule above, your day would currently have four hours for prospecting and selling (assuming you are working eight hours a day). If you fall into the national average for salespeople—ninety productive minutes every eight hours—this means that by applying the boundaries we've just discussed, you can already increase your productive time by 167 percent. Not a bad start.

But we can do even better.

Executive Summary

Serving customers means granting requests, being rather like a genie-in-a-bottle. It means taking on tasks in order to gain rapport and close sales. It takes a big time investment. But most salespeople get themselves swamped because they just can't say no. Or better said, they say yes far too often. This creates a constant influx of wants, needs, and obligations that causes your river of responsibilities to rise high and fast.

Some of these tasks are simply a waste of time and need to be avoided. Other tasks are *necessary* if you want to maintain a high level of customer service. The best way to gain control of your fast current of *necessary* responsibilities is to place more boundaries on your time or, metaphorically speaking, to raise your dam higher. This includes regulating the time you invest in:

1. paperwork;
2. planning and goal setting;
3. surveying customers;
4. observing and evaluating your productivity; and
5. communicating with customers.

This is the second phase of task management and is referred to as damming your Admission of *necessary* tasks.

Chapter Five

The Control Trap
Wasting Time Hoarding Tasks

Master carries heavy burden . . . Sméagol knows. Sméagol carried burden many years.

—GOLLUM FROM *THE LORD OF THE RINGS* TRILOGY

Whether a man is burdened by power or enjoys power; whether he is trapped by responsibility or made free by it; whether he is moved by other people and outer forces or moves them—this is the essence of leadership.

—THEODORE WHITE

The man who is director of half a dozen railroads and three or four manufacturing companies, or who tries at one and the same time to work a farm, a factory, a line of street cars, a political party and a store, rarely amounts to anything.

—ANDREW CARNEGIE

S everal years ago, I was the president, sales rep, accountant, marketing rep, writer, and speaker of the Duncan Group. I had my hands on everything, and the company was growing at a rate of 2.5

percent a year. To be honest, the company's success was hardly worth mentioning—but I felt in control.

Then one day I met with my friend John, a very successful writer and speaker, with two *New York Times* best sellers under his belt and three thriving companies. Four years earlier, he left a flourishing career to pursue speaking and writing full-time. Since I had made the same leap, I wanted to get his take on things. How had he done so well? What were his secrets? How did he manage to take an enterprise he started in a friend's garage and develop it into two multimillion-dollar companies and one successful foundation? Furthermore, what was I doing wrong?

John wasted no time. He immediately told me I was shooting myself in the foot by trying to do it all myself. My success was being stifled, suffocated. There was only so much time in a day, he reminded me, and only so much I could do in that allotment of time. Therefore, the more tasks I controlled, the lower my ceiling of potential fell. He suggested that the only way to grow my business was to raise my ceiling, or, in other words, to lift some responsibility off my shoulders.

I hated to admit it, but I was a bona fide control freak. It was the main reason my business wasn't growing the way I wanted it to, the way John's had. I was trying to expand a sales-based business with two hands and one mind—it wasn't enough. I was guilty of buying into some common misconceptions that essentially caged in my potential:

◆ If I want it done right, I have to do it myself.

◆ No one will work harder for me than I will.

◆ I cannot expect another person to take responsibility for my business.

◆ I am the only one I can truly trust with my livelihood.

My story is fairly common: what begins as an ambitious act of taking ownership often ends up as an unexpected (and often overlooked) burden that weighs us down, a lid that keeps us from rising higher in our endeavors and realizing our potential. It's a frequent mistake in the sales profession, because salespeople are the quintessential self-starters of the working mass. Aren't we the ones who have to pull up our bootstraps, take control of our futures, and make this job "our baby"? Yes, we are—but we *can* take it too far. And when we do, we end up trapped by the very things we try to control.

HOLDING ON TOO TIGHTLY

In the jolly land of the Shire, there was once a well-meaning hobbit named Sméagol. If you've seen the first two installments of *The Lord of the Rings* trilogy, you're probably more familiar with his bug-eyed, skeletal alter ego, Gollum. But in Peter Jackson's adaptation of the final installment, *The Return of the King*, we are flashed back to the story's beginning, and it explains a lot of things, particularly Gollum's seemingly cursed existence.

The film begins with a young Sméagol and his cousin Déagol sitting in a small wooden boat on the river Anduin, surrounded by the lush green landscape of the Shire. Suddenly, Déagol's face lights up.

"Sméagol! I've got one! I've got a fish, Sméag!"

Both chuckle, and Sméagol watches gleefully as his cousin struggles to pull in his catch. As Déagol continues to tussle with his bent pole, the fish at once gives a great tug, yanking him into the water. Sméagol is left gazing anxiously at his cousin's hat as it bobs on the surface. Underwater, a huge fish is pulling Déagol, eyes closed and cheeks puffed with air, along the riverbed. Finally, he lets go of the pole and opens his eyes just in time to catch a flicker of something on the river bottom.

Before kicking to the surface, he closes his hand over a patch of sand.

As he reemerges and begins to climb ashore, Déagol peers back into the shimmering water, and then, remembering something, opens his clenched, muddy hand and gazes at his discovery—a shiny gold ring.

In the background, nervous birds abandon their trees as Sméagol hurries to his cousin.

"Déagol! Déagol!" Sméagol approaches from behind and peers over his cousin's shoulder, eyeing the glistening ring.

"Give us that, Déagol, my love."

Déagol closes his fist and turns to face Sméagol.

"Why?"

"Because it's my birthday, and I wants it."

Sméagol's smile fades slowly—then he snatches at the ring. Déagol dodges his attempt as the two laugh nervously and begin to circle each other. Sméagol lunges for the ring again, becoming less playful. Soon the two are in an all-out skirmish. Sméagol bites at Déagol's arm and the ring falls to the ground. Both scramble madly along the ground, but with a final lunge Déagol grabs hold of the ring then turns and closes five fingers around his cousin's throat. Sméagol lets out a scream and something snaps inside him. His face turns pale and obstinate. Slowly, emotionlessly, he reaches down and closes ten fingers around Déagol's throat and presses firmly from above him. There is only a brief struggle. Sméagol climbs over Déagol's lifeless body and takes the ring from his loose fist. He fingers it close to his face, then, as he slips it onto his finger, he whispers in a guttural voice, *"My preciousss."*[1]

LETTING GO

Some things, if they're not let go, begin to control us, or worse, they begin to consume our time. The longer we hold on, the firmer they ensnare us—eventually they take us down. If the scene ended there, we might be left to assume that Sméagol was only a murderous thief and the ring merely a valuable treasure. But there is more to the ring and more in store for the one who holds it too tightly. If you've seen the trilogy, you know that the ring Sméagol claimed as his own eventually begins to control him and ultimately destroys his life. It's the eventual fate of the control freak.

There are four basic reasons we maintain control even when it's detrimental to our success:

1. Ego—*No one can do it better than me.*

2. Insecurity—*If someone does it better than me, I will look bad.*

3. Naïveté—*I'm fine by myself; I don't need anyone else.*

4. Temperament—*Working with others is too complicated.*

In sales, I understand that your business is your baby. You want to have a firm grasp on its direction and on the things that dictate its fate. But to realize your potential, you cannot hold on too tightly.

There are limits to the value of control. Limits that, if crossed, can impart more damage than delight.

In the course of your career, there are things you should control and things you should not. There are things you should make your baby— your *Preciousss*—and things you must let go of if you are to ever break through the ceiling of average. That is the trap, you see. You must take control of your sales business if you want it to take off; you must take responsibility for its direction—but if you wield *too much* control, you stifle your potential and kill your momentum.

TIME TO FOCUS

Success in any endeavor is a result of focused time. Rocky goes to the mountains of Siberia to train for Ivan Drago. Alejandro Murrieta takes to a cave with his mentor to learn the ways of Zorro. Rannulph Junuh learns to "see the field" and gets his swing back. And Billy Chapel "closes the mechanism" and pitches a perfect game. To become great at anything, you have to learn to focus your time on the main things— the more time you focus on one action, the more proficient and productive you will become at that action. Study any person throughout history who has achieved greatness and see if I am not right about this.

Success in any endeavor is a result of focused time.

This makes more sense when you understand that there is a compounding value to time. Multiple deposits of time on the same tasks can have a big effect. You experience this truth when you invest an hour at the gym each day for a few months. Over time, your sleep patterns will improve, your body will crave better foods, and you will look better physically and feel better emotionally. Invest regular deposits of time in a customer and you'll reap the full value of the relationship through repeat business and referrals you might not have otherwise received.

Conversely, there is very little value in haphazard deposits of time. When you haven't worked out for several weeks, it will do you no good to spend three hours in the gym in one day. You cannot make up for lost time. You can't get in better shape by working out once every three months. Single deposits of time here and there have very little value. This is why multitasking is so unproductive. If all you have time for is arbitrarily servicing the needs of customers as they arise, you will never reap the full value of their business. That's an inconsistent, reactive approach to task management, and more is required if you want to climb out of the swamp and maintain a high level of success.

THE RENAISSANCE IS HISTORY

Even Leonardo da Vinci's life is a testimony to this. I've read much about the original Renaissance man, and it's true that he was good at many things. He had many hobbies. His friends claimed he had the voice of an angel and was also a superb athlete, a brilliant mathematician, and an accomplished scientist. But despite his many talents, by what achievement is he known today? Only one. And as it happens, it is on the pursuit of his art that he focused the overwhelming majority of his time. He understood that greatness is a function of focused time.

To realize your selling potential, you must get in the habit of focusing your time on only the few tasks that bring you the greatest return in business, and then let go of the rest. In your case that means two things:

◆ *building trust with the right prospects*
◆ *adding value to existing customers*

83

—and that requires that you lose some control over other important (even productive) tasks. It won't necessarily be easy, but it's unavoidable if you are to reach new heights in your business.

TAKING FOCUSED ACTION

In the last two chapters we discussed how to dam your Accumulation of *unnecessary* tasks so they will never enter your river of responsibilities. Essentially, this is the skill of interruption management—removing the possibility of needless disruption. We then discussed how to regulate the Admission of *necessary*-but-not-productive tasks to your daily schedule. This is the skill of prioritization—maximizing your time on the highest priorities and minimizing your time on the lowest priorities. These are the two primary skills you must learn and develop in order to clear up your time for the most productive tasks. These two skills will dam your river of responsibilities and keep the current of tasks relatively manageable. But the river can still get out of control if you don't know how to focus the time you've freed up on what's most important.

Phase 3: Action

Once you've set up boundaries that allow you to dam the (1) Accumulation of *unnecessary* tasks and regulate the (2) Admission of *necessary* tasks to your schedule, you must take (3) Action on your most *productive* tasks. Therein lies the problem for many salespeople.

Even if you've built a sturdy dam that blocks unnecessary and unproductive tasks from your river, you can still get flooded with the amount of *productive* tasks you have left to carry out.

With the schedule we've been creating, you've dammed your river enough to give yourself four hours a day to focus on your main productive tasks. Let's take a look at it again.

Time	Monday	Tuesday	Wednesday	Thursday	Friday
9:00	Communication	Communication	Communication	Communication	Communication
9:30	Paperwork	Paperwork	Paperwork	Paperwork	Paperwork
10:00	Main Tasks	Main Tasks	Main Tasks	Main Tasks	Main Tasks
10:30	Main Tasks	Main Tasks	Main Tasks	Main Tasks	Main Tasks
11:00	Communication	Communication	Communication	Communication	Communication
11:30	Paperwork	Paperwork	Paperwork	Paperwork	Paperwork
12:00	Main Tasks	Main Tasks	Main Tasks	Main Tasks	Main Tasks
12:30	Main Tasks	Main Tasks	Main Tasks	Main Tasks	Main Tasks
1:00	Communication	Communication	Communication	Communication	Communication
1:30	Paperwork	Paperwork	Paperwork	Paperwork	Paperwork
2:00	Main Tasks	Main Tasks	Main Tasks	Main Tasks	Main Tasks
2:30	Main Tasks	Main Tasks	Main Tasks	Main Tasks	Main Tasks
3:00	Communication	Communication	Communication	Communication	Communication
3:30	Paperwork	Paperwork	Paperwork	Paperwork	Paperwork
4:00	Main Tasks	Main Tasks	Main Tasks	Main Tasks	Main Tasks
4:30	Main Tasks	Main Tasks	Main Tasks	Main Tasks	Main Tasks
5:00					

The problem lies in the fact that there's more to your two main tasks (prospecting and selling) than calling someone up and shaking someone's hand. We'd all be millionaires if that's all it took. To build trust with the right prospects and add value to customers the right way takes many steps, more than you can handle all by yourself.

In my last book, *Killing the Sale*, I diagrammed the key steps to closing a sale. I want to share those with you here because it serves as a reminder of just how much is involved in selling effectively.

When you look at it this way, it's easy to see that even when you've cleared up time for *productive* tasks, you can still become swamped. Your dam may be regulating the tasks that shouldn't be filling your time, but if you can't properly utilize the time you have left, you haven't made much progress. Water will back up and eventually rise over the dam, making you just as flooded as you were before.

To be successful with your productive time, you need to construct a top

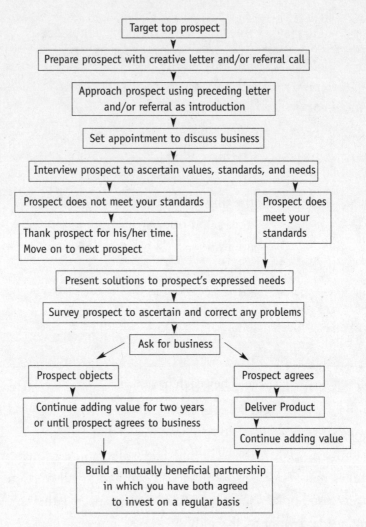

Target top prospect

Prepare prospect with creative letter and/or referral call

Approach prospect using preceding letter and/or referral as introduction

Set appointment to discuss business

Interview prospect to ascertain values, standards, and needs

Prospect does not meet your standards

Prospect does meet your standards

Thank prospect for his/her time. Move on to next prospect

Present solutions to prospect's expressed needs

Survey prospect to ascertain and correct any problems

Ask for business

Prospect objects

Prospect agrees

Continue adding value for two years or until prospect agrees to business

Deliver Product

Continue adding value

Build a mutually beneficial partnership in which you have both agreed to invest on a regular basis

level on your dam. But this level must have a spillway that allows *some* productive tasks to pass through your dam—but not *all* of them.

LETTING GO AND LIFTING UP YOUR BUSINESS

When you're a good salesperson, business can come in like a flood. And when it does, you're going to be gasping for air once again if you try to handle it all by yourself.

Sure, if you multiply the steps I diagrammed above by only three customers, you could probably manage every task yourself, and that's how it is when we're first starting off. We are in control and don't feel overwhelmed yet. But when you begin to grow your business, the rules change quickly; soon you're flooded with more tasks than you have time for in a day. It doesn't take much business either. For instance, in most sales industries, if you multiply the above steps by ten customers or one hundred, you can easily become one swamped workaholic if you are the only one carrying out the tasks.

The truth of the matter is that one is too small a number to achieve greatness in sales.[2] You cannot manage your river of responsibilities alone, especially when business starts to rise. There will come a point (you're probably there already) when you can't handle all the business you create. You need help to contend with the downstream current of success.

At the time of my conversation with John, I was employing anywhere from five to seven people. They each had a job title, but their job descriptions varied with the wind and hinged on what I didn't mind someone else controlling. I held on to the most important tasks. Most of my employees' tasks were menial and involved making calls I didn't want to make or following paperwork trails that ended on my desk in the form of a report or confirmation. Phones were busy and paperwork was everywhere all the time—it was more like a newsroom than a corporate office, and I thought it was productive. But after John's candid advice, I immediately began making changes that freed up my time to focus on my main task—speaking. Today, the annual growth of the company (46 percent) is nearly twenty times greater than it was back then.

The following steps are based on the advice my friend gave me and are the keys to focusing your time and talents on the one or two tasks that bring you the greatest return in business. Not only will the steps multiply your potential for success, they will make it easier for you to achieve more by working less. To construct the third and final level of your dam, do these things:

1. *Answer the 100% question.* While thus far we've managed to free up four hours of your day to prospect and sell, your goal should be to spend the entire day, every day you work, on your top two productive tasks—this is the essence of the 100% question. Of course, there will be other *productive* tasks that pass through your dam, and I will discuss how to manage those in a moment. For now you need to determine how you can best spend your time if given the opportunity. Ask yourself what your business would look like if you spent 100 percent of your work hours doing the two things that brought the greatest return to your business. How much more could you make? How much less stress would you have? How much less would you have to work? How much better would your life be off the job?

Of course, you will not maintain this standard overnight, but by visualizing its results, you will find it easier to make the necessary decisions to get there—and those are forthcoming in the remainder of this book. For now, so that you comprehend the value of this question, here's a snapshot of a salesperson who sought out the 100% standard, gave up some control, and gained the freedom it offers:

> *Your goal should be to spend the entire day, every day you work, on your top two productive tasks.*

	Before	After
Chuck:	70 hours a week	40 hours a week
	15 sales a month	40 sales a month
	2 weeks of vacation	10 weeks of vacation
	1 location, solo effort	3 locations, a team of 18

2. *Assume a CEO mind-set.* When I considered this step, the irony was that I was already the CEO of the Duncan Group. The problem was that I wasn't acting like it. A CEO mind-set is looking at your sales job as you would if you were the owner of a company and then determining what decisions need to be made to grow and to ensure future stability. A CEO realizes that in order to take a sales business to the next level and keep it growing, you must invest time (and eventually money) in the fertile ground of (1) productive customer relationships, and (2) productive business relationships. When you see your job as a company you've been hired to run and grow, some important variables become clear—namely, the necessity of good help that allows you to focus on what's important.

3. *Delegate in increments.* If we're honest, even with your interruptions at bay and productivity climbing, four hours a day is hardly enough time to complete every *productive* task that comes our way, especially when sales are raining down like a waterfall. All salespeople eventually come to a place where they accept that they must do one of two things:

1. work more hours; or

2. let sales and customer service slide.

Most don't consider the third option:

3. seek help from other people.

I'm not telling you to immediately go out and hire an assistant. Some of you may not be able to afford it just yet. Since it is *your* business (CEO mind-set), the initial investments you make and the level of risk are up to you. However, there are incremental steps that will help you work up to hiring an assistant and eventually a team. And these are necessary if you desire to maximize your time and potential.

Take a look at these four delegation steps and determine at what point you should begin sharing some of your workload.

Delegation Step 1: *Hire yourself.* Essentially, you've already done this by blocking four hours a day to take care of *necessary*-but-not-productive tasks. During these four hours (or whatever amount you've decided on) you act as your own assistant. For some, this alone might make a huge difference in your success. But this is only the start, as four hours a day is a lot of time to give to tasks that don't directly affect the bottom line—especially when you consider that those hours could be used for the most productive tasks.

Delegation Step 2: *Utilize the help your company provides.* This is something often overlooked and underused. Many salespeople are employed by companies who already pay people to take care of some of the *necessary* tasks that you are carrying out. Before you consider what it would take to hire your own help, consider what help is available to you from your company. You might be pleasantly surprised.

I highly advise that you get your manager involved at this point. Request a short meeting to discuss your new productivity goals and what the company has to offer in the way of help. Even if your company has no in-house assistance available, letting your manager know that you are actively taking steps to focus your time on increasing sales will be pleasing to hear. Furthermore, this conversation will lay the groundwork for your next step.

Delegation Step 3: *Hire a part-time assistant.* You have four hours of work each day that needs to get done but is not the most productive use of your time. If you delegated these tasks to an assistant, you'd only have to pay him or her for twenty hours a week. At this point, the importance of the CEO mind-set really sets in. Some of you may be scoffing at the idea of hiring an assistant with your own money or having to train one, but if you're really interested in blowing the lid off your potential, this is a necessary investment. And you need to see it that way—as an *investment*.

Remember Tim, from the beginning of the book? You know—the one who was faxing his life away. Well, this was his first step in letting go of some necessary tasks, and the way he did it was very effective.

Tim met with his manager and offered a deal: he would pay for his own part-time assistant for six months, and if after that period of time his sales had increased enough to cover the cost of the assistant, the company would hire her. The manager agreed. And you know what? After only three months, Tim's increased sales were already deferring the cost of his assistant, and the company took over the cost, convinced of her value to Tim's productivity. By the way, Tim now has six assistants.

When you consider the return on investment that a part-time assistant can bring, the decision is much easier to make. For instance, if you hire an assistant for four hours a day at (let's start modestly) $10 an hour, you'd spend $200 a week for his or her services. It sounds like a lot if you're making $1,000 a week, but consider the return. You will have four more hours a day to spend on your top two productive tasks. If you only close one more sale a week with this extra time, and you make $500 in commission per sale, you've just increased your income by $300 a week or $1,200 a month. That's a 30 percent increase right away, with only one more sale per week.

If you are paid less per sale, this formula still works well. Generally speaking, the more time you have to sell, the more you will sell. If you consider the return on investment from strictly a time standpoint, you can fairly assume that if you are currently spending four hours a day on your top two productive tasks and earning, say, $100 a day in total commissions, with an assistant you will be able to double your productive time to eight hours a day, and reasonably double your total daily earnings to $200. Even if you're paying an assistant $40 a day, you're still making an additional $60 a day, which translates into a 60 percent increase in commissions.

Sure, your sales results will vary from month to month depending on some factors that may be out of your control, but that doesn't nullify the point that hiring an assistant is a small price to pay for doubling the amount of time you can spend on productive tasks. If you really feel you cannot afford the cost right now, consider sharing a part-time assistant with a coworker whose values you share. This will cut the cost in half and still free up ten more hours a week for you to sell. That's a start. And when you immediately begin to reap the benefits, you'll probably wonder why you didn't do it sooner.

Now, there's something else I want you to consider—in fact, you've already begun. It has everything to do with the fact that most of us would probably work less, much less, if we knew we could still increase our success and earn a better living than we are now.

Delegation Step 4: *Begin building a team.*

When I met Harry, he was like Sméagol—he hoarded everything for himself. He employed a few people who simply took messages and scheduled tasks, but they didn't return calls or carry out any real work; that, according to Harry, was *his* baby. Then, at one of my events, he was struck with what he calls a "blinding flash of the obvious."

With a team, the sky is the limit.

As I was sharing with the audience the bleak realities of being a control freak, Harry realized that he had been severely stifling his selling potential by keeping his hands on every important task. He was showing up to work early in the morning, at six or seven o'clock, and working until seven every night, with at least one week-end day to get caught up. A lot of hours, in other words. Needless to say, he was the wrong kind of busy—a bona fide control freak, like I was.

When Harry returned home, inspired from my event, he sat down and began to list what should be delegated. He then had his employees shadow him throughout the day to learn every aspect of his job. Before long, each of them could handle every task that might arise, including the most productive tasks.

Today, Harry's team of four literally runs the show. He spends every minute of his time building trust with prospects and adding value to existing customers. Everything else is taken care of, and that has nearly cut his working hours in half and affords him stress-free vacations whenever he wants them. And in case you're wondering, his income has increased 400 percent since letting go. What Harry learned is that with a team, the sky is the limit.

When you're ready to initiate this final delegation step, here are the four things your team needs to succeed:

1. *A team needs a purpose to excite them.* If you've seen the film *The Rookie* you'll remember the key scene in the movie, where his team confronts Dennis Quaid, playing high-school baseball coach and former minor-league pitcher Jim Morris, about his ability to pitch. They strike up a deal with their coach that if they win their league title, he has to try out for the majors. It's the stimulation the team needs to succeed. When you begin building a team, make sure you give them something exciting to strive for that's as valuable to them as their help is to you.

2. ***A team needs an opportunity to gel.*** "Houston, we have a problem," says Tom Hanks in the film *Apollo 13*. He's playing the astronaut Jim Lovell, who has just discovered that fuel is leaking out of the spacecraft at a rapid rate. If Houston wondered how they would work together when it really mattered, their question was about to be answered. In the end, the team proves it has what it takes. The only way your team will gel is by having some big responsibilities. It's your job to give them the chance to come through.

3. ***A team needs a coach to empower them.*** Russell Crowe speaks power to his fellow gladiators by leading them "as one!" to their first victory in the Colosseum. Once you begin building a team, your role is to give your players the means to succeed. This requires you to define their roles, train them thoroughly, and encourage them often. If they fail and you haven't done your job, their failure is your fault.

4. ***A team needs intimacy, honesty, and accountability to unite them.*** You might recall this scene if you've watched the film *Remember the Titans:* Denzel Washington, playing Coach Boone, is faced with the reality of leading an interracial football team in a segregated time. He takes the team on a mandatory morning run to the Gettysburg battlefield, where young men lost their lives fighting for the same thing—racial equality. The team is forced to come to terms with their issues, and eventually unites as brothers. In the same way, set your team standards up front and hold each member accountable for their actions—good and bad. This is the best way to ensure unified success.

TAKE THE FIRST STEP

For some of you, building a team is a couple of steps away. For some of you, spending half a day on productive tasks is *huge*, a giant step forward. And you should go with that. Start where you need to and work your way up. But don't quit halfway because, trust me, it doesn't take long for the rewards of this stuff to kick in. I've always said that *if you have a dream and don't have a team, your dream will die. But with a team, your dream will fly.*

Some of the ideas in this chapter may seem revolutionary—even ridiculous—given your circumstances. For instance, if you work out of a cubicle, it would be a little odd (and a little too cozy) to squeeze an assistant in there with you for half the day. And then there are your company's rules and liability issues, etc., etc. These are some of the things you may have to take into account as you strive to maximize the value of your productive time. Like any endeavor toward success, there will be hurdles, and that's okay. My advice is to think outside the box and get your boss involved from the outset. When your boss understands what you are trying to do, he or she will more than likely be willing to help you take the necessary steps—even if it requires doing something out of the ordinary. At the very least, he or she won't be surprised by anything you try to do. Put together your best selling skills and make it your goal to get your boss on your side with this stuff. And if you want, like Tim, make an offer your boss would be a fool to refuse.

> *If you have a dream and don't have a team, your dream will die. But with a team, your dream will fly.*

The encouraging news is that once you work your way to hiring an assistant—even if you're sharing one with a coworker—you will have already taken the first step toward building a team. And that is literally the beginning of the end for your days of being swamped.

But there's one more phase we need to work through in order to maximize your productive time. With the dam behind us, we now need to assess your capacity to be productive . . . because there are still a few hindrances that can slow your raft and delay your progress downriver.

Executive Summary

In the course of a sales career there are things you should control, and things you should not. There are things you should make "your baby," and others things you must let go of if you are to ever break through the ceiling of average. You must take control of the most productive aspects of your sales business if you want it to take off, but if you wield *too much* control you stifle your potential and kill your momentum. And that's because success in any endeavor is a result of focused time.

To realize your selling potential, get in the habit of focusing your time on only the few tasks that bring you the greatest return in business. Let go of the rest. That means investing your time in two things:

◆ *Building trust with the right prospects*
◆ *Adding value to existing customers*

Give up control over other important (even productive) tasks by seeking the help of others.

◆ Answer the 100% question.
◆ Assume a CEO mind-set.
◆ Delegate tasks in increments.
◆ Begin building a team.

These steps conclude the construction of your dam and constitute the third phase of task management referred to as taking focused action on the most *productive* tasks.

Chapter Six

The Technology Trap

Wasting Time on Time-Saving Devices

My assistant says I'm hard to get a hold of, but I just counted: She has eight ways to get in touch with me. There's my cell phone that's always with me, but sometimes the battery goes dead. Then there's my work phone, but the voice mailbox gets filled up pretty quickly. Then there are my two home numbers for which I have several cordless phones; the reception gets fuzzy only when I'm in the back half of the house. My wife's cell is usually on, and if I'm with her, she can reach me there—although her ringer is sometimes off. I have two e-mail addresses that I check when I'm in the office, which is about ten hours a week, but currently only one of them receives e-mail. The other one is for emergencies only. And then there's my PDA—it's wireless . . . I don't understand what the problem is.

—TODD DUNCAN

During a period that we now call the Enlightenment, Sir Francis Bacon described a modern civilization that would emerge if we unleashed the power of science and technology. This unleashing, he was convinced, was the path to a society of unprecedented convenience, choice, well-being, and prosperity for all people. In 1624, he called this technological island paradise the New Atlantis. Today we call it America.

According to biographer William Hepworth Dixon, "Every man who rides in a train, who sends a telegram, who follows a steam plough, who sits in an easy chair, who crosses the channel or the Atlantic, who eats a good dinner, who enjoys a beautiful garden, or undergoes a painless surgical operation, owes [Bacon] something."[1] That was written in 1862. Nearly 150 years later, we might have Francis Bacon to thank for something else. I call it the Technology Trap, but it's been called by many other names. Maybe you've heard of them.

The computer. The laptop. The Internet. The PDA. The CrackBerry. The cell phone. The pager (although it's sooo last season). E-mail. V-mail. The wireless router for your wireless laptop with a wireless card in it. The Wi-Fi for your PDA that allows you to check e-mail and v-mail from anywhere. The flash memory that makes your cell phone a stereo, video game, and camera in one. You get the picture.

Bacon led us to science, science led us to technology, and technology led us to the wonders of time-saving devices. But these days, the devices we laud as efficient may be stealing the very thing they were designed to save.

THE TIME BANDITS OF TECHNOLOGY

I have nothing against technology. I'm not a Marxist, and I don't think machines are eventually going to replace humans in the labor force. Technological advances have done wonders for the world and will continue to do so. But in an ever-expanding era of gigabytes, Web sites, and satellites, many of us have become a little gadget happy. As a result, we may be losing more time with technology than the time we intend to gain.

In a *Seattle Times* article titled "Saving Time No Longer a Tech Reality," columnist Paul Andrews asks the question, "Has technology become a time bandit?"

Part of the workday involves dealing with technology. That's where the concept of time thievery comes in. Bandits include computers, voice mail, e-mail, the Internet and automated processes where humans have been supplanted by technology.

I thought of time thievery the other day at the supermarket, where shoppers can now check out, pay for, and bag their own groceries. You stand at a kiosk and pass your bar-coded groceries through scanners, which somehow also recognize fruit and other noncoded items. If I were in a hurry, self-checkout might be a way to avoid standing in line . . . [But] if supermarkets start requiring all shoppers to do self-checkout I won't be saving myself *any* time. There will be lines at the kiosks just as there are today at the checkout stands.

Plenty of other examples abound . . . I can remember when I began using PCs back in the early 1980s. They saved me enormous amounts of time. And e-mail was a wondrous advance over the drudgery of appropriately named snail mail. Fast forward to today's perception of PCs. Perhaps 2003's most notorious time bandits are the twin evils of spam and Windows viruses. If one isn't clogging our in-box, the other is crashing our PC.[2]

I can certainly relate.

Last year, when my writer, Brent, and I were working on *Killing the Sale*, his laptop got infected with a virus, and he couldn't access any of his files.[3] He spent over *twenty hours* on the phone with a tech expert over the course of two weeks. When I asked him how it was finally solved, he said it wasn't. After reinstalling the hard drive three times, the tech expert gave up and ordered him a new motherboard— if you don't know, that's the equivalent of a new laptop without the plastic casing. And because of those two weeks spent in a technology trap, the book was completed after the original deadline.

This year, it was something different, but the story is the same.

Brent purchased a new laptop, hoping to avoid any major setbacks, and he did—but of course, there is still *my* laptop.

Awhile ago my e-mail crashed several days in a row, leaving Brent without important feedback from me for several days—one time, when I was on the road, he was without my correspondence for almost two weeks. This once again hurried our writing schedule.

Unfortunately, the Technology Trap is a regular and universal problem, because even the most basic amenities can tie us down and steal our time.

Take e-mail, for starters.

While e-mail has offered us an efficiency of communication that we never knew before, when we consider the setbacks that can plague us over the course of a day, it may prove to add more stress than time to our days—my recent experience illustrates this. I'm sure you could think of an experience of your own—maybe as recent as today.

The problematic potential of e-mail has become so great that a recent *USA Today* article began with these words: "For years, consumers and corporations raved about e-mail's potential. Now they're fretting about its future."

According to the article, our cyberfrustrations cost us over $15 billion in personal losses and workplace productivity last year alone. It cites the three most prevalent e-mail ailments and the huge costs associated with each. I think we can relate to every one of them. Take a look:

Spam
(Unsolicited e-mails that plague your in-box)
The stats: According to national e-mail monitoring company Brightmail, in the month of May [2004] about 64 percent of all e-mail was spam—up from 58 percent in December of last year.

The cost: "It costs companies nearly $2,000 per employee a year in lost productivity, double from a year ago," says Nucleus Research. On average, spam alone results in a loss of about 3.1 percent of total productivity.

Phishing
(Spam that tricks consumers into surrendering their personal information)

The stats: "Phishing attacks soared to a record 1,125 unique schemes in April [2004] . . . according to the Anti-Phishing Working Group."

The cost: Each attack can add anywhere from 50,000 to 10 million e-mail messages to or from your in-box.

Viruses
(Self-replicating programs that harm files and slow processor speed)

The stats: There are currently 90,800 known viruses in cyberspace with the potential of infecting your computer each time you open an e-mail or surf the Internet.

The cost: If they're not crashing your computer or blocking access to important files, many viruses leave "security holes" in your computer, allowing hackers to remotely send spam and phishing schemes to you and others from your computer. This includes your prospects, coworkers, and trusted customers.[4]

About five years ago, reality set in. The tribulations of computer technology were costing us big time. Computer Economics in Carlsbad, California, reported that businesses worldwide lost a total of $7.6 billion in revenue and productivity in the first two quarters of 1999, at the hands of Melissa, the Explore.Zip worm, and other viruses.[5] This certainly led to a global increase in computer security funding within corporations.

Today we're not only spending more time dealing with these dilemmas; we are spending more revenue.

According to *Entrepreneur* magazine, if our technology dilemmas continue at their current pace, the Radicati Group estimates that revenue and productivity losses from computer viruses "will reach $75 billion in 2007 worldwide—up from $28 billion [in 2003]." Radicati also estimates that by 2007, individuals and corporations will spend $6.1 billion for antivirus solutions and $2.4 billion for antispam and content-filtering solutions—up from $1.8 billion and $653 million in 2003.[6]

Of course, we can talk in general, global terms about the time traps people get into with technology, but the reality is that if it doesn't affect us personally, we don't see the problem.

However, I'll be the first to admit that it does, in more ways than one. I have a feeling you're in the same boat.

During a recent workout, I noticed a Boeing commercial that began with the words: "Freedom rises on the wings of technology." I had been having trouble with my laptop, and I remember thinking, *The only thing rising on* my *wings of technology is frustration.*

And the challenges continue, not just for me but for everyone around me . . . as I'm sure you can easily imagine.

TECHNICAL DIFFICULTIES . . . PLEASE STAND BY

In an airline's frequent-flyer lounge, I recently asked why I had two membership cards. "One is for our new magnetic reader," the lady behind the counter explained. "But it isn't working due to technical difficulties. It will eventually replace your old card, but we can't use it yet."

Halfway through that same trip, I overheard another traveler telling the person on the other end of the phone that he had just spent thirty minutes trying to figure out how to adjust the volume on his cell phone. He ended the conversation by saying, "Let me call you back on a landline."

The other day I showed up at my friend's house, and he was completely frustrated. When I asked him what was wrong, he said, "I've spent half the day trying to figure out how to use this new camera. It claims it's supposed to do everything—except teach you how to use it, I guess."

Another friend owns a sales business, and they're trying to convert everything to wireless technology. It's been fourteen days, and it's still not working.

A few months ago, I sat in a meeting with a few people from my publisher's office. They asked how this book on time was coming along. I told them fine, as long as we didn't fall into any more traps. Everyone laughed—then someone admitted to having 619 unopened e-mails.

Technology traps are everywhere, and we fall into them every day. They not only keep us constantly connected to our jobs, making us slaves to others' schedules; they cut deeply into our time. Too often technology is a hindrance instead of a help. I don't think there's any question about that. But one question that needs asking is this: *Can a solution for technology be found with more technology?*

By our actions we assume it can. Why are we almost *compelled* to purchase the latest, greatest edition of a technotool we already own?

CAN TECHNOLOGY SOLVE ITSELF?

It's as though we think technology will at some point be flawless, without glitches and bugs. But our loftiest expectations are unfounded. Technology will never be perfect; it's created and maintained by people—flawed people, I might add. The fact is, until people are perfect, technology won't be. But that doesn't seem to stop us from expecting technology to purge itself of its problems.

Even the government fell victim to this misunderstanding. Earlier this year, Congress sought out a technosolution to a technoproblem when it proposed a national do-not-spam registry to follow in the wake of the do-not-call registry offered last year. But according to *USA Today*, the Federal Trade Commission threw cold water on the idea, stating that it would likely lead to more spam and greater vulnerability for users of e-mail. Furthermore, the FTC noted that managing a list with up to 450 million addresses would be a technological nightmare.[7]

Technology is not its own solution—it never will be. And that's because technology is not the problem. We are.

In conclusion to his article, *Seattle Times* columnist Paul Andrews reminds us, "To be sure, technology is not the culprit—technology is just a tool. But in many ways, it's become a tool the user can no longer control. Perhaps in addition to 'Take Back Your Time' [day], there should be a 'Take Back Your Tech' day to remind us of technology's original benefits and to strategize overcoming its abuses."

Spam, phishing, viruses, poor cell reception, and wireless hiccups will always exist. Technology is designed and advanced by men and women, and it will therefore remain fallible. A cell phone that gets perfect reception everywhere you go? Never. We'll always ask, "Can you hear me now?" E-mails will still slip through the cracks, computers will still get viruses and crash, PDAs will still fail to sync, and wireless technology will still only work so far from wires. The problem isn't technology; the problem is our unreasonable expectations of it and our dependence on it.

If we start there, a solution to the Technology Trap is within reach.

REGAINING CONTROL OF TECHNOLOGY

I have to admit, I have been the first in line to buy the latest techno-tool more than once. I want it to improve my productivity and help me be more effective at what I do. And honestly, it often does. But there are also moments—too often to count—when technology fails me and usurps my time. It's in those moments that I realize I need to be more strategic about how I use technology.

I'm not advocating that we all toss our hardware in a fire pit and douse it with gasoline. I just want you to see that making the most of your now-freed-up work time requires that you put some parameters on your use of technology.

Phase 4: Assessment

I believe there are actions we can take in order to temper the Technology Traps that so often sap our productive time. Remember, we're on a river, and the dam is now behind us. We've done a good job thus far in damming the many tasks that normally flood our time and keep us unproductive. We've freed up at least half your day to prospect and sell—or your entire day if you are able to delegate to an assistant or team. If you apply what we've discussed thus far, you can expect a much smoother ride downriver.

But as you know, even when your time is freed up to prospect and sell, you can still squander it needlessly. That's because even when the current is calm, there are still burdens that can weigh down your raft and slow your progress. Technology is one of the most common burdens we bear because we rely on it so heavily to prospect and sell.

Nevertheless, it *can* be good thing—as long as you know how to keep technology from impeding your progress. Here are five ways to accomplish this:

1. *Shorten the leash.* At my High Trust Sales Academy™ events, I appoint one attendee to be the pager and cell phone "sheriff." I then tell everyone in attendance that if a cell rings while I'm on stage, the owner has to pay a fine to the sheriff on the spot: $20 for a first offense, $40

for a second offense, and $100 for a third offense. Any money that is collected over the course of the three-day event is donated to a charity that the audience has voted on. You wouldn't believe how big the pot swells. At a recent event the attendees set a new record, doling out over $1,200 in fines—several people donated on more than one occasion. You'd think the attendees would just turn their pagers and phones off—but many don't. And usually it's because they're afraid they'll miss an important call. Unfortunately, they are not set up to break free from their technological leashes.

With most of us carrying at least two of the three—a cell phone, a laptop, and a PDA—we are attached to work twenty-four hours a day. As a doctor, police officer, or firefighter, this level of availability is necessary. For you, it's not. In fact, it's usually detrimental. One of the biggest traps of technology is the ability it gives us to work anywhere, anytime. I'm not sure which is truer: technology keeps us on top of things, or it keeps things on top of us. Only you know the truth. But when the latter is more accurate, you need to shorten your leash and give yourself time free from the threat of work interruptions. Otherwise, two things will continue to happen: You will never maximize productivity on the job, and the life for which you are working may never exist.

2. *Substitute, don't stockpile.* According to *Newsweek*, "There are 1.5 billion mobile phones in the world today. Already you can use them to browse the Web, take pictures, send e-mail, and play games. Soon they could make your PC obsolete."[8] I hope so, because the fewer tools we rely on to accomplish our work, the better. Will we ever have one technotool that will allow us to do everything? Not anytime soon. But the closer we can get to it, the better off we'll all be.

When you add up all the time you lose with technology problems, it makes sense to use your tools only as needed and not in unnecessary excess. You know what I mean. We buy techno tools all the time that we don't really need. Or we buy a new version of something we already have and continue to use the old one as well as the new. *If you have to buy a new piece of equipment, get rid of your old one; don't try to use both.* Substitute, don't stockpile. Donate your old cell phone to a women's shelter, where they can be used for emergencies. Give your old computer to a nonprofit company or a college student you know. Let a coworker or customer have your old PDA. Use what saves you time, and do away with the tools you've replaced. Technology can save time, but there comes a point when the more you have, the less time you save.

3. *Ask directions.* Guys don't ask for directions, I know. And women usually do. So maybe this particular piece of advice is more for my male readers. Either way, if you want to waste a ton of time, try to figure out how to use your techno tool on your own. I just spent seven hours trying to learn how to use an MP3 player. It was a tool I bought because I can download lessons from the Web and listen to them on the road without having to keep track of several CDs. Not to mention it's much easier to carry than a portable CD player. But because I didn't know how to use the thing, I was seven hours in the red from the start. I should've taken advantage of the salesperson's knowledge and let him teach me. It would've taken fifteen minutes. Then I would have been saving time from the get-go. Instead, MP3 technology has created a deficit of time.

There's nothing genius about this piece of advice, but so few people use it. We buy techno tools and take hours teaching ourselves to use them—this is a major time sapper. Then, to compound the problem, we never figure out how to use all the functions with which we could ultimately save more time. How many functions on your PDA or cell phone or laptop do you not know how to use? See what I mean? Too often, we make the false assumption that technology automatically equals time saved, when the truth is that it only saves us time if we know how to use it effectively. The quicker you get to that place, the sooner you start saving time.

4. *Test your tools' efficiency.* Four years ago, I spent big bucks for a very nice laptop. The thing had everything I thought I might need to get my job done efficiently at home or on the road. It had floppy, zip, and CD drives, a fifteen-inch screen, and a top-of-the-line sound system with all the function buttons above the keyboard. It was heavy, but I figured it was a small price to pay for having an all-in-one computer that would increase my productivity. About three months later, I realized that I didn't use half of what the laptop offered. Now I was stuck lugging around this ten-pound box that was beginning to become a burden. In fact, I stopped taking it with me, because I dreaded carrying the thing. Besides that, I realized that all the software on it required a ton of memory and made it function slower.

In the end, I gave the laptop to a friend who works from a home office and doesn't travel, and I bought a small laptop that offered only what I needed. I've been using it effectively ever since.

We all need to evaluate the efficiency of our technological tools. And we need to be honest about what we discover. Don't keep something that just looks good but that gives you all kinds of trouble or has many useless functions. Don't hold on to something that doesn't do what it's supposed to do. It's wasting your time. Take your time researching the tool you feel will give you the biggest boost in time, and then test it out. If it's a success, great—stay with it. If it's slowing you down, dump it for something that makes more sense. And don't rule out the option of doing things the old-fashioned way. Technology isn't always more efficient than you.

5. *Go backward to go forward.* I recently sat in a meeting that concluded with the scheduling of another meeting. As soon as a date was

mentioned, everyone checked their calendars. "I'm available on that date," I replied, as I looked up from my paper calendar that is filled out in pencil. It was silent as everyone else mashed buttons and poked wands at their PDAs. About a minute later, they all chimed in that they were free.

How free is another question.

Sometimes technology isn't better. It's just prettier. I know that there's a subtle pressure to have the hippest tools available. But if you can accomplish something more efficiently without a tool, don't get a gadget because everyone else has one. Besides, retro is in these days. It's a fashion trend in clothing, cars, and housewares. Why can't it be in technology too?

> *Sometimes technology isn't better. It's just prettier.*

LIGHTEN THE LOAD

When it comes to time and technology, we would do well to remember the tortoise and the hare. So often we play the hare, with our flashy, fast-paced tools designed to save us time and get us from point A to B much quicker, but which only slow us down in the end. We need to heed the advice of the tortoise, who always tended toward a slower but more deliberate pace. It wasn't that the tortoise didn't want to go faster—he just understood the only way to do something right is to sacrifice some time on the front end to figure out the right path, and then move forward confidently and purposefully to the finish line. This is our lesson with technology, and it is our lesson from here on out: the essence of the Assessment Phase is trading time on the front end to reap more time on the back end.

You see, the truth is that you can free up all the time in the world to grow your business; but if you don't know how to use that time effectively, you can still waste much of your days—and that may be worse after all.

It's bad enough to be swamped with tasks that needlessly fill your time and put a lid on your success—but you know how to overcome that now. It's even worse to have enough time to succeed, but squander it away in the name of productivity and efficiency. Misused technology is often the cause of this, but there are other reasons. Let's assess them one at a time. In the end, with a dam behind us and a steady current before us, we'll be smooth sailing.

Executive Summary

The Enlightenment led us to science, science led us to technology, and technology led us to the wonders of time-saving devices. But these days, the devices we laud as efficient may be stealing the very thing they were designed to save. But technology is not the problem—we are. Many of us have become a little gadget happy, losing more time with technology than we gain.

We've done a good job thus far in damming or regulating the many tasks that normally flood your time and keep you unproductive. We've freed up at least half your day to focus on your most *productive* tasks (or your entire day, if you are able to delegate to an assistant or team). But even when your time is freed up to prospect and sell, you can still squander it needlessly. That's because even when the current is calm, there are still burdens that can weigh down your raft and slow your progress. Technology is one of the most common burdens, because most rely on it heavily to prospect and sell. Nevertheless, it *can* be good thing—as long as you keep it from impeding your progress. There are five ways to accomplish this:

1. Shorten your technology leash.
2. Substitute your technology devices, don't stockpile them.
3. Ask directions for maximizing your technology tools.
4. Test your technology tools' efficiency.
5. Go backward to go forward; don't use technology if an old, manual method is more efficient.

These steps represent the final phase of task management called the Assessment Phase. In this phase you are assessing your use of the time you've freed up and removing any hindrances to your productivity.

Chapter Seven

The Quota Trap
Wasting Time Counting Sales

I started selling only what I knew worked, because I couldn't lie
anymore—so my managers told me to either close more deals or
find another job.

—MATT COOPER
SALES AND MARKETING
MANAGEMENT

People who've been selling for years are earning about the same
hourly wage that fresh college graduates make without a day of
sales experience.

—TODD DUNCAN

We constructed boundaries to eliminate your (1) Accumulation of *unnecessary* tasks. This phase helped you get rid of needless time interruptions. Then we constructed higher boundaries to regulate the (2) Admission of *necessary* tasks to your schedule. This phase helped you free up four hours a day to be productive. Next we discussed the necessity of taking focused (3) Action on the most important *productive* tasks by relinquishing some control of other important tasks to an assistant or team. These three phases completed the construction of your dam and not only tamed the chaotic current of your river, but also freed up at least half your time to prospect and sell—this is likely two or three times more than you had before. But remember, having time to sell is one thing—being highly productive with that time is another.

That brought us to the fourth and final phase of task management.

The Assessment Phase is about being highly productive during the time you've freed up with your dam. It begins when you understand how to use but not abuse technology—when you learn to avoid the Technology Traps that are everywhere in today's society. The next step in the Assessment Phase is to avoid something I call the Quota Trap.

Let me explain this as we now move forward.

The Value of Time

It was Ben Franklin who originally claimed that "time is money," and he understood something that's often lost in today's fast-paced marketplace—but not by everyone.

Visit a lawyer or mechanic and you'll see what I mean. You will exchange money for a service—but that's not all you're paying for.

Spend a few hours with a lawyer and you may receive a few legal documents and some official signatures that help you settle a case. But when you get the bill, you will know that you're being charged for more than a few slivers of bark and a couple of teaspoons of ink. You will know you are paying for the lawyer's time—more so, in fact, than for anything else.

Take your car to get that whistling sound fixed and you'll be charged for two things: the new parts the mechanic installs, and his time. As I'm sure you know, the longer the work takes, the more you will be charged. That's because the mechanic's time is more valuable than the parts he installs. A mechanic understands that without his time, all you have is a whistling car and a pile of metal parts. So he charges you according to the value he places on that time.

In essence, the lawyer and the mechanic understand that there is more to a business transaction than exchanging money for a product or service. There is also the exchanging of money for time. It's a truth all swamped salespeople need to be reminded of.

TRADING TIME

The custom of trading has been around since the beginning of time. In fact, before currency existed, it was how individuals obtained what they needed to live. If winter was coming and I needed some warm garments, I might offer you some crops from my field in exchange for a few furs. If you wanted a gift for someone and I was hungry, I might offer you a necklace of beads for a portion of meat. That was then.

Today we might observe that modern society rarely trades on an individual level out of *necessity* unless it's merely a favor for a favor. But that's only our observation if we don't consider time as a commodity.

Sure, most salespeople would admit that time has value. The problem is that we never really distill what that value is. But when you look at time as a defined commodity—something that we trade for a negotiated return—you begin to understand the implications of spending it in unproductive or haphazard ways. I've found that most salespeople trade their time for far too cheap a return.

WHAT'S YOUR GOING RATE?

Have you ever thought about what your time is worth? If you were only paid by the hour, what would you charge a customer for your time? Wait, don't answer that. The truth is that your hourly rate is already determined whether you know it or not.

It's a simple equation. Take the amount of money you've made over the course of the last twelve weeks and divide it by the amount of hours you've worked over that same period. The equation looks like this (fill in your own numbers here):

$$\frac{\$\rule{1cm}{0.4pt} \text{ (Total income for last 12 weeks)}}{\rule{2cm}{0.4pt} \text{ (Total hours worked for last 12 weeks)}} = \$\rule{1cm}{0.4pt} \textbf{ per hour}$$

By the way, it does you no good to fudge your numbers. We're trying to maximize the value of the time you've freed up thus far, and that requires that you be completely honest about *all* the hours you invested in work, including time on the phone and the Internet over the weekend, etc. It also requires you to be truthful about the money you have *already collected*—not the money that *should* come in later.

When most swamped salespeople I've worked with tally their hourly rates they are surprised at how little they work for—especially when I give them something to compare it to.

For instance, let's say you averaged 70 hours a week for the last twelve weeks, which means you spent a total of 840 hours working for the quarter. And let's say you made an average of $5,000 a month so that your income for the quarter was $15,000. You might be tempted to think you didn't do too badly, but when you break it down into an hourly wage, it becomes clear that you're not exactly coming out on the good end of the deal.

When you divide your quarterly income ($15,000) by your quarterly hours worked (840 hours), you come up with an hourly rate of only $17.86/hour. To give you a frame of reference, according to

CareerPrep.com, if you applied for a sales job fresh out of college last year, you could expect to earn, on average, about $19.09/hour—and this during what many called a minor recession.[1]

It's unfortunate, but I've found that most swamped salespeople work for somewhere between $10 and $20 an hour. In other words, people who've been working for years, sometimes more than ten years—persons not just in their twenties and thirties, but their forties and even fifties—are earning about the same hourly wage that fresh college graduates make without a day of sales experience.

What does *your* current hourly rate say about how you've been trading your time?

WASTING TIME COUNTING SALES

Most salespeople trade their time far too cheaply, and I've found it's primarily a result of one thing: the quota.

In yesteryear, the traveling salesman was a respected individual; in fact, it's what most men my grandfather's and father's ages did for a career. There may have been mention of quotas back then—more as goals than requirements—but they weren't necessary. Steady competition, personal dignity, and family responsibility set the standards and inspired traveling salesmen to trade their time well and succeed.

Nowadays, personal and familial standards are much lower, and distractions are aplenty. With competition, greed, and fear of job loss often the only forces compelling us to succeed, quotas can be used like whips on our backs, driving us to produce a certain quantity of sales but fooling us into ignoring the quality of our time. As a result, selling standards hit the dirt, productivity takes on a deficient meaning, and salespeople resort to desperate measures to hit their numbers and keep their jobs. Matt Cooper was one of these people.

In a recent *Sales and Marketing Management* article, Erin Strout reveals Cooper's ugly discoveries about today's unrealistic expectations placed on salespeople and how it ultimately affects their productivity.[2]

> For Matt Cooper, the cost of earning up to $150,000 per sale was spending every day lying to his customers. It was the promise of huge bonus checks—not his $40,000 base salary—that lured him to join the sales force of a large, well-known Internet company two years ago . . . but what he didn't realize was that dishonesty was the price of admission. The New York-based start-up formed a big-deals team, a group that sold multimillion-dollar advertising campaigns to some of the world's largest companies. The sales force's key strategy? Do whatever it took to close those deals . . . "If you didn't lie you were fired," Cooper says. "It always came down to careful wording and fudging numbers."

Cooper admitted to Strout he was forced to lie nearly 100 percent of the time. Another rep working with Cooper confessed, "We might have sold all of our telecommunications inventory, but then another company would call to say they wanted to spend $50,000 on a campaign. What would we do? Book it, even though all the space had already been sold. When the numbers didn't come back as high as the customer expected, we'd just chalk it up to a bad campaign. We'd take anybody who was willing to spend a dime."

As a result of his deceitful tactics to meet his quotas, one customer whom Matt Cooper swindled out of more than $1 million began leaving him increasingly hostile messages. Eventually, the customer threatened his life. "He left a message saying, 'I know you're there. I'm going to find out where you live and blow up your house.'" According to Strout, Cooper never spoke to the customer again and left the sticky situation in the hands of the company. He also admitted that something similar happened a few other times.

Finally, he couldn't take it anymore. Admitted Cooper, "I started selling only what I knew worked, because I couldn't lie anymore—so my managers told me to either close more deals or find another job." Essentially they told him he was wasting company time if he wasn't closing sales *their* way. The irony is that just the opposite was true. Nevertheless, Cooper took the high road and moved on, chalking up the wasted time as a lesson learned.

Not so long ago, Matt Cooper's story would have been rare and disturbing. Today, it's almost commonplace. In fact, a survey conducted for the article by *SMM* and Equation Research revealed that 47 percent of sales managers suspect their salespeople lie during sales transactions. But is it merely out of their hunger for money and success that salespeople sink to such shameful tactics? It's easy to assume so. But the majority of sales managers say it's not the main reason. According to the survey, "Seventy-four percent admitted the drive to achieve [unrealistic] sales targets encourages salespeople to lose focus on what the customer really needs." In other words, salespeople succumb to substandard sales tactics because their current practices aren't productive enough to meet their quotas.

THE QUOTA QUANDARY

Unfortunately, because quotas tempt us toward speedy (and even seedy) selling tactics, they often make us counterproductive with our time. For example:

- Quotas may increase your pace, but they decrease your focus.
- Quotas may increase your action, but they decrease your assessment.

◆ Quotas may increase your exposure, but they decrease your effectiveness.

◆ Quotas may increase your short-term turnover, but they decrease your long-term trust.

◆ Quotas may increase your short-term production, but they decrease your long-term profitability.

Quotas are too often the driving force behind a salesperson's strategy. The problem with that is it can persuade you into thinking that *quantity* of sales is the most important factor in success. This often compels you to ignore the quality of your customers, which significantly decreases the value of your time over the long haul.

If you are motivated to meet a quota, you are compelled to sell to any- and everybody that comes along—whether or not they're a good fit. Like the furniture salesman who craftily followed two ladies to the back of the showroom, hoping to catch them at the peak of their curiosity. He caught them, all right—one was breastfeeding her child, and the other was asking him if he was an idiot.

As a result of haphazard and hurried selling strategies, you end up with a majority of customers who never return or refer anyone else to you. Trapped, you must then rely on new business—on full-time prospecting—to achieve any degree of success. This always means more time spent for less business in return. It's a poor trade-off.

However, when meeting a quota isn't your motor of productivity, it's an entirely different story.

In her article, Erin Strout spoke with Brett Villeneuve, the operations manager at Go Daddy Software, who says that he purposely hires reps that are less money-driven and more relationship-oriented. Villeneuve understands that the value of a salesperson's time is not based on sales numbers. It is based on the total return for the time invested.

True productivity = All business received over time ÷ All time invested

When you subscribe to this definition of productivity—whether or not your manager does—you've taken the first step toward reaping the most value for your selling time, and in doing so, eliminating the pressure you feel to constantly meet a quota.

GETTING MORE FOR YOUR TRADE

Let's not forget how far we've come. We've freed up a minimum of four hours a day to work on your most productive tasks: prospecting and selling.

Time	Monday	Tuesday	Wednesday	Thursday	Friday
9:00	*Communication*	*Communication*	*Communication*	*Communication*	*Communication*
9:30	*Paperwork*	*Paperwork*	*Paperwork*	*Paperwork*	*Paperwork*
10:00	Main Tasks	Main Tasks	Main Tasks	Main Tasks	Main Tasks
10:30	Main Tasks	Main Tasks	Main Tasks	Main Tasks	Main Tasks
11:00	*Communication*	*Communication*	*Communication*	*Communication*	*Communication*
11:30	*Paperwork*	*Paperwork*	*Paperwork*	*Paperwork*	*Paperwork*
12:00	Main Tasks	Main Tasks	Main Tasks	Main Tasks	Main Tasks
12:30	Main Tasks	Main Tasks	Main Tasks	Main Tasks	Main Tasks
1:00	*Communication*	*Communication*	*Communication*	*Communication*	*Communication*
1:30	*Paperwork*	*Paperwork*	*Paperwork*	*Paperwork*	*Paperwork*
2:00	Main Tasks	Main Tasks	Main Tasks	Main Tasks	Main Tasks
2:30	Main Tasks	Main Tasks	Main Tasks	Main Tasks	Main Tasks
3:00	*Communication*	*Communication*	*Communication*	*Communication*	*Communication*
3:30	*Paperwork*	*Paperwork*	*Paperwork*	*Paperwork*	*Paperwork*
4:00	Main Tasks	Main Tasks	Main Tasks	Main Tasks	Main Tasks
4:30	Main Tasks	Main Tasks	Main Tasks	Main Tasks	Main Tasks
5:00					

But as we now know, having the *time* to be productive is one thing; *being productive* with that time is another—especially when the constant pressure of quotas is involved.

Removing the burden of a quota requires that you produce more business in either the same amount of time you are currently working or, ideally, in less time than you are currently working. From an hourly rate perspective, here is what the before and after might look like if you only increased your income but kept working the same amount of hours:

Before

$15,000 *(Total income for last 3 months)*

$$\frac{\$15,000 \text{ (Total income for last 3 months)}}{840 \text{ (Total hours worked for last 3 months)}} = \$17.86/\text{hour (Hourly rate)}$$

840 *(Total hours worked for last 3 months)*

After

$25,000 *(Total income for last 3 months)*

$$\frac{\$25,000 \text{ (Total income for last 3 months)}}{840 \text{ (Total hours worked for last 3 months)}} = \$29.76/\text{hour (Hourly rate)}$$

840 *(Total hours worked for last 3 months)*

Most "time management" gurus will only show you how to accomplish a greater return from your time by teaching you the art of getting organized and focusing, which by nature decreases the amount of time you must work to produce the same income. In the same example, if you worked ten hours less per week over the twelve-week period, it would look like this:

$$\frac{\$15,000 \text{ (Total income for last 3 months)}}{720 \text{ (Total hours worked for last 3 months)}} = \$20.83/\text{hour (Hourly rate)}$$

This is only one step in the "becoming more productive" process—one, in fact, that you've already taken in the previous chapters—but it's not the most effective step, nor is it the final step. That's because there's always a limiting factor involved. You. Even if you're the most organized, get-it-done, do-it-now salesperson on the planet, there is still a limit to the amount of customers you can see and sales you can close in a given period of time. There's only so much selling you can accomplish each hour. In short, your productivity will eventually plateau if all you do is get more focused and better organized. And if meeting a quota requires more than you can do in eight highly organized, strictly focused hours a day, you are still stuck working longer hours under constant pressure to perform. (And let's face it, we all know most quotas are a bit unrealistic and would be difficult to meet even if we were highly focused and organized.)

We've done our best to clean up your time—we've gone as far as most "time management" experts will take you—but we must go further to maximize the value of your time trade-offs each day. The only other way this can happen is by increasing the value of what you receive for your time, in other words, trading your time for a higher-valued customer. Doing this will quell your quota worries for good.

GETTING *EVEN MORE* FOR YOUR TRADE

By trading your time for only high-value customers, you can increase your income without increasing your time. In other words, you can trade the same amount of time (or less, as you'll see) and get more business in return.

David's story is a testimony that this is very possible. He runs a sales force of eighty-eight salespeople and had for years overlooked the value of teaching his team to only pursue the top customers in their market. His salespeople weren't unskilled or underhanded, but they were for the most part taking a haphazard approach to selling, and it wasn't reaping the returns he had hoped. Then he took my advice and implemented a new training program for his salespeople that took into primary account selling to only the most valuable customers in the market. He taught them whom to—and whom not to—pursue. This one change in strategy immediately boosted his team's sales. Not only that, his salespeople admitted they suffered far less stress and felt much less pressure to rush. In short, they had time to sell the right way to the right people, and it made a 300 percent difference.

You can imagine how that changed the future of David's career. But consider how the simple change in strategy brightened the future of every one of his salespeople. Less stress, less pressure, less time . . . and *more* productivity? That's not a bad trade-off, is it?

To realize the success that David's salespeople have, you must follow their same strategy. The steps they took and continue to take today are the keys to maximizing your productivity while *minimizing* your time on the job.

TRADING TIME FOR TOP CUSTOMERS

There are four general categories that define all customers, no matter what industry you're in. When I shared these with one client named John, he made changes immediately to whom he prospected and in only eight weeks received business from thirty-three new, top-quality customers. To begin trading your time for the highest return, you must understand who the *best* customers are—because, trust me, not everyone is worth your time:

High-Maintenance/Low-Profit

Customers that fit this description have low potential for business and are very hard to serve because of unrealistic price and service demands and/or inefficient business practices. It's obviously in your best interest to avoid trading your time with such customers. To do so is like investing two hours in a customer who's interested in buying a pair of socks. Don't waste your time; it's more valuable than that.

High-Maintenance/High-Profit

Customers that fit this description have the potential to produce a lot of business but are very difficult to serve, also because of unrealistic price and service demands, as well as inefficient business practices and a high need for ego fulfillment. Generally speaking, these customers expect more than you can give them and don't relent until they get what they want. It's like the Mercedes customer who wants you to woo him for two months because he thinks he deserves it, then waffles on price and threatens to take his business elsewhere if you don't comply with his desires. Don't waste your time with such customers. Instead, invest time in the next two types of customers.

Low-Maintenance/Low-Profit

Prospects in this category have the potential to produce little business but are likely to provide greater profits as the relationship grows. Furthermore, they are easy to serve because of a high level of professionalism, a desire to partner with you, and efficient business practices. This makes them a wise investment. My experience is that as you invest little bits of time consistently with these types of customers, their appreciation will grow and they will be more than happy to send their friends and family to you. A few years ago, my company finalized a seven-figure, multiyear contract with a customer we had been courting for over three years. They had given us a little business over that time, but we knew that once we established ourselves as trustworthy and capable of exceeding their expectations, the value of the return would increase significantly—and obviously it did. The goal with low-maintenance/low-profit customers is to move them over time into the final category. We'll talk about an effective, time-sensitive strategy to accomplish this, but first let's discuss the final and most important category of customers.

Low-Maintenance/High-Profit

Customers that fit this description are the ones in which you want to invest the majority of your time. They will trade you the most business for the smallest investment of your time. That's because the customers in this category have one overarching commonality. A few years ago I sat next to a fellow business author on a plane back to our homes in San Diego, and he explained it this way. He said that the most successful sales relationships have a common "essence." Both you and the customer understand the purpose of the relationship, agree on the direction of the relationship, and share the same personal and professional values in order to grow the relationship. Relationships of this nature rarely fall into your lap. Most often, these customers must be groomed and courted in order to receive their maximum value. But once they have given you business, the idea is to hold on to them for life. That's where your time trade-off becomes a highly lucrative deal.

GETTING THE FULL VALUE FOR YOUR TIME

Once you understand who is worth your time and then begin to pursue only those types of customers, there are four strategies you need to maintain in order to maximize the value of your prospecting time.[3]

1. *Prequalify prospects before you pursue them.* You may be working from a list of already-prequalified leads, but that's not what I'm talking about here. When I say "prequalify prospects," I mean that *you* need to determine whether the people you call on are fit for an

investment of your time . . . before you call on them. This may mean you need to dump your company's list and start your own. You have resources you may not realize, and I know you're a bright person, because you bought this book. To begin a list of qualified prospects ask the question, *whom do I know who knows who I need to know?* All prospecting lists should begin with that question. My brother Jeff is a successful financial planner. For years he never asked me for referrals. Then one day we met and discussed his business. Not only did I remind him of this truth, but we devised several ways for me to refer him some clients. Within a week, he was doing business with the top salesman at a dealership where I buy my cars. You will be surprised at how many prospects you already have a connection to. And remember that current customers and friends are often the best resource for new prospects.

2. *Never call on a prospect unexpectedly.* A coworker named John gave me this piece of advice when I was first starting out in sales, and it's always stuck with me. He told me that I should never call on a prospect that isn't expecting my call or that isn't excited to talk to me. In other words, if my prospects didn't know who I was or why I wanted to speak with them, I was wasting my time trying to sell them anything—and so are you. There are many ways to warm up a prospect before calling on him, but in my experience, here are the most successful:

- ◆ Send a value-added approach letter that evokes a sense of curiosity and makes you memorable.

- ◆ Have a common friend or colleague introduce you over the phone or in person.

- ◆ Have a common friend or colleague arrange a meeting.

3. *Cut ties with time-consuming customers*. This includes high-maintenance prospects. If you find that you are already investing time in someone that fits that description, you need to cut ties professionally and with integrity. Use a script similar to this:

> *Ms. Jones, I have spent some time evaluating my business, and I have come to the conclusion that I cannot give you the level of service that you desire from your vendor relationships. Rather than modify my whole system, I'd like to thank you for your business and encourage you to find a supplier that can serve you the way you would like to be served.*

I know saying this to a customer will strike fear into some of you, and that's perfectly normal. It's not easy to terminate an unproductive sales relationship, because no one likes confrontation. But you must realize that if you're serious about maximizing the time you've freed up, you have to trade your time with only the best customers—and that may require you to stop trading time with customers who take much time and give little business in return. The reason former faxaholic Tim can work only eighty days a year and make a ton of money is because he focuses his time on serving the needs of only twelve customers who bring him all the repeat and referral business he wants. Fewer deep relationships are more valuable and less time-consuming than many shallow ones.

Fewer deep relationships are more valuable and less time-consuming than many shallow ones.

4. *Transition relationships into partnerships*. Most salespeople have no idea how much a customer relationship is worth over a long period, so they typically invest more time in new relationships instead of current ones—but that's a poor trade-off. Thomas knows this, and that's why he is one of the best sales professionals I know. He works for Fletcher Jones Motor Cars in Newport Beach. I travel over ninety minutes from where I live and pass six dealerships selling the same cars to give my business to Thomas. Why? He knows the value of a lifetime customer, and it keeps me coming back. The birthday calls are great. The postcards from overseas show me he cares. Sending me pictures of future models keeps me excited. In short, he's regularly on my mind. Here's what Thomas knows:

The High-End Auto Customer

A. The average commission amount	$1,000
B. Number of sales per buyer every three years	1/3
C. Revenue per year (A x B)	$330
D. Client life cycle	20 years
E. Client value over life cycle (C x D)	$6,600
F. Average client referrals per year	4
G. Value of client referrals per year	$1,320
H. Revenue if first-year referrals close and reach life cycle	$26,400

Total Lifetime Value of One Auto Client (E + H)	**$33,000**

You might look at that and think, *So what's the big deal? It's not that much to lose.* But what if you missed out on this value with every customer because you were too busy trying to secure new business? Then what would you lose? I'll tell you. If you failed to go deeper with only ten clients in one year, you would miss out on $330,000 over the course of twenty years. Or if you fail to go deeper with, say, two hundred customers over the course of a year, that amounts to $6.6 million lost over twenty years or $330,000 a year. If you want to retire early—or at least have that option—you don't want to miss out on the full value of customers. Sure, these numbers are big. But to be honest, they're not unrealistic. Take a look at what the top salesperson in your industry is making and see if that doesn't convince you that there is money to be made if you know how to make it.

The greatest time you can trade is not in constantly seeking new business but in deepening your current customer relationships. A few years ago, a client named Linda began following this philosophy, and she now has one customer who accounts for about $750,000 in sales revenue *every month*. Do you think she'd rather deal with fifty separate customers to realize that same return? You need the right customers to be hugely successful.

I don't want you to think that I'm telling you to never prospect. What I want you to see is that prospecting is not the *best* investment of your time, and the most successful salespeople—those who spend the least amount of time earning the most amount of money—are the ones who have transitioned from an acquisition-based business to a retention-based business that only invests time in prospecting when . . .

◆ entering a new market,

◆ expanding their business, or

◆ replacing customers who have run full cycle or moved on.

Once you know your customers well and have built trust with them, transitioning to retention-based partnerships will not be difficult; in fact, in most cases customers welcome the change because it represents a greater benefit to them.

That said, there are four surefire steps to transition your customers into lifetime partners:

1. *Take inventory.* Who are your best customers? Who gives you the most return in business for your time? Who are the accompanying players—the customers who give you business, but not as often or as much as the best customers? And which customers don't make the cut? Rank them according to their level of importance in three tiers, with the number of customers in the top level accounting for 60 percent of your business, the number of customers in the second level accounting for 20 percent of your business, and the number of customers in the third level accounting for 20 percent of your business. If you currently have twenty customers, here's what it might look like:

Client Ranking	% of Your Total Revenue	# of Customers
VIP Level	60%	4
Premier Level	20%	6
Standard Level	20%	10

2. *Determine the amount of time you will invest on a regular basis back into your three levels of customers.* It's important that you be proactive about trading your time with current customers, because it will eventually alleviate your need to prospect. This will keep you in constant control of your river. The Pareto Principle suggests that about 80 percent of your business comes from the top 20 percent of your customers—in this example, that means the top ten customers. Therefore, it makes the most sense for you to invest 80 percent of your time back into these top ten customers and give the remaining 20 percent to the customers in the Standard Level in an effort to raise them to a higher level over time. Using the same example as above, if we take the four hours a day that we've freed up with your dam, your strategy will break down like this:

Ranking	% of Revenue	# of Customers	$ Invested Back	% of Time to Invest
VIP Level	60%	4	15% of revenue	60% (144 mins/day)
Premier Level	20%	6	10% of revenue	20% (48 mins/day)
Standard Level	20%	10	5% of revenue	20% (48 mins/day)

I realize that the allotted time to invest each day may not seem like a lot, but you have to understand that you won't invest time in every customer on every day. The idea is to set up a regular contact schedule that tells you who to invest time in each day, week, or month.

3. *Determine your annual contact plan.* Set up your contacts with customers strategically so that you are fostering deeper relationships that will lead to a continual stream of repeat and referral business. You can create your own schedule based on how much prospecting you need to do and how many customers you currently have, but in general, here are my suggested parameters for regular contact with each level (it is best if these meetings are informal and are conducted away from the office in a restaurant or café):

◆ For VIP-Level customers, you should invest a minimum of two hours every month in face-to-face time or phone-to-phone time, shaping and evaluating the goals of your partnership and deepening your relationship. I personally call 200 of our best customers each month.

◆ For Premier-Level customers, you should invest two hours every quarter in a face-to-face meeting and five more thirty-minute meetings (phone or face-to-face) over the course of the year, for a total of nine.

◆ For Standard-Level customers, you should invest two hours in a face-to-face meeting once a year to discuss the goals of the partnership, then thirty minutes every quarter in informal meetings over the phone or face-to-face.

The goal of your regular contact schedule is to grow your relationships in each level so that, eventually, you are receiving steady repeat and referral business from each customer. It should be noted that these scheduled time investments do not include necessary calls or meetings for the purpose of discussing referrals and sales—those you should schedule as they arise, letting them replace prospecting time.

With four hours a day to invest in current customers (and four more hours to use for necessary communication and paperwork), you will have plenty of time to do what you need to do.

Remember that if you still need to spend time prospecting at this point in your career (and many of you will), you should insert prospects into the bottom levels until you have enough customers to occupy all your time. Be careful not to rely on prospecting for too long—there will come a certain point when you have to wean yourself off the prospecting bottle and rely on your system of partnerships to give you business. Believe me, seeking retention business is a much better investment of your time than trying to rely on acquisition to sustain success. The basic weaning formula is to invest your scheduled time each day with current customers and their referrals, and then invest any leftover time in prospecting until you are receiving enough business from current customers to occupy all your time.

4. *Finally, cast your vision to your customers.* Obviously, you need your customers on the same page with you for all of this to work. On an individual basis, schedule face-to-face meetings (over meals or coffee is okay), and take the following approach in the meeting:

135

◆ First, let them know how much you appreciate their business and desire to continue serving their needs by developing a mutually beneficial partnership.

◆ Second, share how you desire to add value to them—with their direction.

◆ Third, ask them to help you determine how the two of you can compose a mutually beneficial partnership based on the specifics of both what they will receive from you and what you will receive from them.

Keep in mind that if you've been treating your customers poorly, this may not be received well right away. If that's the case, instead of trying to force this on your customers, show them your intentions by investing your time in them for two months without asking for anything in return. Then, when you've built a better rapport, move forward with a partnership-planning meeting.

A MORE ENJOYABLE RIDE

When my writing partner, Brent, was learning to guide, he told me he hated having a full raft. It put more pressure on him and made his mistakes more pronounced. But the more proficient he became and the more confidence he gained, he realized that having a full raft was the best ride of all. More smiles, more laughs, and more satisfied rafters meant more fun and fulfillment for him. And furthermore, when he had the right people in the raft, who were there to have a wonderful experience, it was much easier to guide.

I realize that all of this—or a big part—may be new to you. But don't get overwhelmed and not follow through. These steps are easy to implement and maintain once you get the hang of it. Like Brent's experience guiding on the Klamath, you may lack confidence at first—and that's very normal. But once you get to a place where all your customers are on board with you, your ride down the river will take on new meaning and offer a much grander potential. In fact, if you maintain your dam and follow the strategies we've discussed thus far, eventually three things will happen:

- You will have fewer customers but more income.

- You will be more productive in less time.

- Quotas will never scare you.

When you begin to invest time in the right tasks *and* the right people, you will soon find that eight hours a day is more than enough to maintain a high degree of success. I know this because many of my clients are living proof. The vast majority are working an average of thirty to forty hours a week and taking anywhere from six weeks of vacation to fax-happy Tim's twenty weeks of vacation a year.

When you know *how* to spend your time and with *whom* to spend it, the sales profession doesn't have to flood your days and drown out the important things in your life. In fact, with the right strategies, your sales career can be the catalyst that helps you create the life you may have written off.

You now have the tools and training to do it. Once you construct the boundaries we've discussed and done your best to assess the actions you are taking during your productive time, you are set up to succeed. Now there are only two things that can hamper your progress downriver: failure and success.

Let's talk about failure first.

EXECUTIVE SUMMARY

Most salespeople trade their time for far too cheap a return, many times due to that often unreasonable and inefficient standard of sales success we call the quota.

Because quotas tempt us toward speedy (and even seedy) selling tactics, they often make us counterproductive with our time. For example:

◆ Quotas may increase your pace, but they decrease your focus.

◆ Quotas may increase your action, but they decrease your assessment.

◆ Quotas may increase your exposure, but they decrease your effectiveness.

◆ Quotas may increase your short-term turnover, but they decrease your long-term trust.

◆ Quotas may increase your short-term production, but they decrease your long-term profitability.

The problem with a selling strategy reliant on meeting a quota is that it can persuade you to think that *quantity* of sales is the most important factor in success. This often compels you to ignore the *quality* of your customers, which significantly decreases the value of your time over the long haul. Removing the time-sapping burden of a quota requires that you produce more business in either the same amount of time you are currently working or, ideally, in less time than you are currently working.

Most "time management" gurus only show you how to accomplish a greater return from your time by teaching you the art of getting organized and focused, which by nature decreases the amount of time you must work to produce the same income. It's a step, but not the most effective one. A better way to remove the burden of a quota is by increasing the value of what you receive for your time—trading your time for a higher-valued customer.

Once you understand who is worth your time and pursue only those customers, there are four strategies for maximizing the value of your selling time:

1. Prequalify prospects before you pursue them.

2. Never call on a prospect unexpectedly.

3. Cut ties with time-consuming customers.

4. Transition customer relationships into partnerships.

Following these strategies will result in more income from fewer customers, more productivity in less time, and the removal of quota pressure.

Chapter Eight

The Failure Trap

Wasting Time Worrying About Yesterday

When defeat comes, accept it as a signal that your plans are not sound, rebuild those plans, and set sail once more toward your coveted goal.

— NAPOLEAN HILL

Failure should be our teacher, not our undertaker. Failure is a delay, but not defeat. It is a temporary detour, not a dead-end street.

—WILLIAM WARD

At each of my events, there are at least a half dozen people who approach me to admit how regretful they are that they wasted so much time. Many quantify this by divulging the number of months or years they've wasted. I empathize because I spent about half of my first decade of selling making poor choices, professionally and personally. I worked twelve-plus hours a day; I abused my body with drugs and alcohol; I compromised my integrity to make a buck; I turned my back on my faith; I spent money to make a statement—the more the better . . . I thought I had it all, but I was wrong. I carelessly squandered more time than I can measure.

When I look back on those years, I sometimes shudder at the man and salesman I was. But that is yesterday, and there is nothing I can do to change that period of time. Those years are etched in my personal history and cannot be rewritten. The only story that is still to be penned begins today and ends when God says it does, hopefully many years from now.

It's important that you understand this, because the only time that matters today *is* today. Right now. This moment. There are things you can change and things you cannot. The band Switchfoot wrote a song about this, called "This Is Your Life," and it's a call to move beyond the time you no longer possess and contemplate the time you do:

The only time that matters today is today.

Yesterday is a wrinkle on your forehead
Yesterday is a promise that you've broken
Don't close your eyes, don't close your eyes
This is your life and today is all you've got now
Yeah, and today is all you'll ever have
Don't close your eyes
Don't close your eyes

This is your life, are you who you want to be?
This is your life, are you who you want to be?
This is your life, is it everything you dreamed that it would be
When the world was younger and you had everything to lose?[1]

If past failures slow you down, then failure is a trap that steals time from today. But when you recognize that the only time you can do anything about is the moment you are in now, failure takes on a different meaning.

Taking a cue from my friend John Maxwell, my failure probabilities have diminished greatly by creating my Daily Dozen. Each morning I review these things to help me gain perspective and increase the odds of success. Here they are:

My Faith gives me peace.

My Family gives me harmony and stability.

My Fitness gives me stamina and energy.

My Friends give me counsel and comfort.

My Finances gives me options.

My Future gives me direction.

My Focus gives me growth.

My Feelings shape my attitude.

My Faithfulness gives me serenity.

My Freedom gives me choices.

My Fun gives me renewal.

My Fulfillment gives me joy.

GOOD-BYE TO THE OLD YOU

I know that at this point in the book, you may be looking at your career—and even your life—and thinking, *I can't believe how much time I've wasted. I can't believe I let things get this way . . . I shoulda done this . . . I gotta stop doing that.* A female student was at this same point after the first day of one of my three-day events. She stayed up all night to handwrite an eight-page document she titled "Good-bye to Me." Here are some excerpts from her letter:

June 17, 2004

I am so at the bottom today that the only place I have to go is up. You see, last Monday my boss gave me a verbal warning to shape up or get canned. Do I have circumstances going on in my life? Yes . . . I have let go of so many things: my business, my family, my Christ, my values. Where have I been? My husband left . . . I pushed his buttons . . . I told him I never loved him. I know I did. He was my first true love; we lived so much together. He stopped wanting to achieve . . . and began to not care . . . I guess I walked away too. At first I was angry. Disillusioned. I even harbored resentment . . .

I haven't been happy in years—not sure how long, maybe three years . . . I have been writing my life plan for the last 2 years—I wonder if any other sales coach has been more frustrated as [mine] since he knows me and my potential. I have been promising, overpromising to my kids, my family, myself; and I come up short daily. [This] makes you realize, "Okay, I have short-changed myself daily for many years while having the tools to do all of this correctly. Forget the reasons; forget the excuses. I just wasn't ready to be successful."

Most people this evening worked on their mission statement . . . [Instead] I just wanted to say good-bye to a life lived by accident and reaction. It hasn't been much fun; it's been sad, frustrating, scary. I want to say good-bye to the woman who is ashamed to go to church on Sunday because she is going alone with two kids, the one who doesn't schedule her doctor appointments because she doesn't make her health a priority. I want to allow myself to cry in order to grow . . . I want to place value on my time . . .

The purpose of why I write this letter is to say good-bye to all those things and actions that have not allowed me to reach my fullest potential in life . . . Good-bye, Old Me.

What my client came to understand that day is that, despite all her failures and setbacks, time was still moving on, and therefore, so must she if she was to ever begin working and living as she desired. It's a lesson that many of us need to learn, as hard as it may be.

I imagine you have some misused time you'd like to forget—especially after reading this book. Maybe it's time for you to say good-bye to the old you, let go of the time you cannot change, and begin giving yourself fully to the time you still possess.

THE PARADOX OF FAILURE

To overcome failure we've been taught to be persistent . . . take initiative . . . be aggressive . . . stick to it, and eventually we will gain the confidence to succeed more often. But the truth is that overcoming failure takes more than mental toughness and fervent initiative. It takes more than an ability to avoid or ignore your setbacks. Overcoming failure takes perspective.

Mistakes are inevitable in every profession, but especially in the sales profession. I know, because as a salesperson I made my share. One time I failed to send some important paperwork to a client on time, and she called to let me know of her frustration. I could have stopped at one mistake, but I was on a roll. Instead of apologizing and trying to better the situation, I became defensive. Quickly (and quite understandably, I might add), her frustration elevated to anger. She told me how awful I was being and threatened to take her business elsewhere. I told her to go ahead, take her business to someone else; I didn't need her business anyway. She hung up and made good on her threat. But the consequences didn't stop there. In less than a week I received word from four other customers that they would no longer need my business. Word had spread about my actions, and they didn't like what they heard. In the end, instead of losing my pride and ego, I lost five customers and a ton of future business.

Salespeople are people, which is to say we are fallible—we're gonna make mistakes, and we don't need another person to help us. But we have help nonetheless. We are around other people all the time—other fallible people. And not just around them but in their faces and engaging in conversations with them, and in their wallets and purses, and sometimes in their personal lives. To the chagrin of some, sales is not an individualistic enterprise. Not many jobs are. The sales profession is fallible salespeople offering fallible products to fallible customers. It's a breeding ground for blunders, and many of us are quite fertile.

I don't intend to make light of the ways you have failed. Some of your mistakes may have been costly; you may have squandered years. They may have even been painful. I understand that too. Not that many years ago, I made a poor decision about a business partnership, and it nearly put my company into bankruptcy—and that soured everything else in my life. After investing years to move my business upward, I fell close to the bottom in a matter of minutes. The ripples of that mistake took years to subside. But I've moved on. Since then, there have been other mistakes as well, but thankfully with less taxing results. What I want you to see is that nobody succeeds in this business without failure. To use a billiards phrase, nobody runs the table. Everybody fails, even the best.

A MORE EFFICIENT PERSPECTIVE

When asked about an unexpected defeat, tennis great Chris Evert Lloyd said, "If I win several tournaments in a row, I get so confident I'm in a cloud. A loss gets me eager again." She understands that failure has an upside. It's the paradox of failure that many of us miss as salespeople.

A person's emotional progression in response to failure goes something like this:

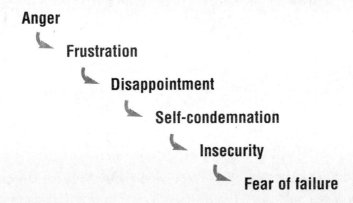

Anger

Frustration

Disappointment

Self-condemnation

Insecurity

Fear of failure

In the beginning of a sales career, it is easy to maintain a high level of enthusiasm and optimism. For some, this can be maintained for a couple of years, despite setbacks. A go-get-'em attitude keeps them hopeful, even if in reality they are hanging on to their jobs by a hair. During this time, the lower negative emotions exist (self-condemnation, insecurity, and fear of failure), but enthusiasm and optimism mask them.

But over time that can change. After multiple failures, enthusiasm begins to wane (as we all know it does) and optimism fades to uncertainty. In short, salespeople begin to feel the full gamut of emotions when they fail. And if a salesperson does nothing to improve this situation, the progression of their emotional response often becomes truncated in a subconscious effort to lighten the blow.

Self-condemnation

Insecurity

Fear

The truth, however, is that the blows of failure only get worse. Each of their three emotions becomes magnified until the salesperson becomes paralyzed, fearful to take any action that might result in failure.

Self-condemnation

↘ **Insecurity**

↘ **Fear**

↘ **Inaction**

This is precisely why nobody likes cold-calling. Sure, it's a challenge at first; but once you make a few dozen calls and have half hang up and the other half tell you they aren't interested, you begin to lose hope. At first you may just feel reluctant about making calls—nobody likes to call a stranger and offer her something she might not even want or need. But after a while, insecurity and fear set in, and you begin to figure out ways to sabotage calls so you don't feel so bad about yourself. Maybe you start your conversations with, "Sorry to bother you, but . . ." or, "I know you're probably not interested, but . . ." You may even start inflating the number of calls you tell your boss you've made. Sooner or later, to keep your job, you figure out who the easy prospects are—the ones that won't make you feel stupid or that you can easily manipulate—and you begin calling only on them. In the end, though it seems to alleviate your anxieties, all this does is delay the inevitable: low productivity and long hours to achieve mediocre success, at best. It's a fate many salespeople suffer. In fact, it's for this very reason that there is so much job turnover in the sales industry.

On the other hand, salespeople with a healthy perspective of failure don't let their emotions go beyond disappointment. Once faced with the reality of failure they adjust their attitude and, with resolve, take the necessary actions to learn from their mistakes and move forward with improved action. Ultimately, such salespeople end up in a better position than when they started.

Improved action

Anger   **Confidence** ↙

   ↘ **Frustration**   **Resolve** ↙

      ↘ **Disappointment** ↙

You see, the paradox of failure is that while it's not the most productive path we can take, it is often the most efficient teacher we can have.

THE EFFICIENCY OF FAILURE

It's easy to get comfortable in our careers. Because sales is a challenging endeavor, we often accept a routine where we say and do the same things in the same ways in order to achieve the same level of success . . . or in order to best avoid failure.

I don't know what your situation looked like before you picked up this book, but I have a feeling you've had to face some past failures in the pages that preceded this one. You've no doubt realized ways that you are being unproductive, and I'm sure that has been frustrating. But in leading you down this path to time freedom, I don't intend to lure you into another trap by showing you your failures and then leaving you to stew in them.

I understand that failure can paralyze us all. And the reality of your failures in this book may have taken a toll on your self-esteem or at least made you feel a little gun-shy about making any changes. If that's true, I'm certain you're not alone. But let me tell you something about failure—it moves you closer to success. While failures certainly slow us down, and, if left unattended, make us completely unproductive, they can ironically speed us up in the long run if we know how to handle them. This is the right perspective I mentioned earlier. The truth about failure is that, while it's never the best use of our time, it can often increase our productivity quicker than anything else. Failure, if perceived right, is the sharpest tool for whittling away our inconsistencies and inefficiencies.

When a client named Dave stopped meeting with his sales coach, he admitted it was primarily for one reason: his coach was prodding him to take steps that he felt were too risky. In the following months after letting his coach go, nothing happened. When I say nothing, I mean nothing different. Dave went about his sales business the same safe way he always had—long hours and mediocre results. He couldn't understand what the trick was to increasing his productivity and sales. Then at an event, I told him he was afraid of failure, and it was holding him back. It was keeping him from doing the things he needed to do to achieve the level of success he desired.

Failure, if perceived right, is the sharpest tool for whittling away our inconsistencies and inefficiencies.

Don't get me wrong; Dave wasn't a sloppy salesman. In fact, he was very thorough and trustworthy. But as many thorough people are, he wasn't into taking risks, and he was untrusting of others to do his work for him. He liked having his ducks in a row and knowing where each duck was headed. He avoided uncertainty. He liked knowing all factors in the equation and the answer ahead of time. As a result, he had reached his limit of productivity. The only way he would improve now, I told him, would be to take some chances. And though it was difficult, he did.

The first risk on his agenda was to rehire his coach. The second risk was much more difficult. He was to hire an assistant. For years Dave had been doing everything himself in an effort to avoid failure. What he didn't realize is that he was only prolonging its effects. Dave reluctantly agreed to take the risk. He did a typically thorough job of screening and interviewing people for the job and finally hired someone he felt was a good fit. Unfortunately, she wasn't. After a month it became clear that he needed to hire someone else. Dave was upset. He had taken a risk, and, just as he expected, he'd gotten burned. It was difficult, but with some encouragement, he tried again. He took new applicants through the interview process and hired a new assistant. And you know what? She liked the work so much that she decided to apply for a sales position, leaving Dave once again without an assistant. But instead of stewing in his self-fulfilled prophecy again, Dave refused to quit. By this time he had seen the value of an assistant, and he immediately hired another, his third in a few months. And this time it was a perfect fit.

If I ended the story there, the lesson would be simple: don't let the fear of failure keep you down. But remember we're talking about time, and there's an even happier ending to Dave's story. It is true that because Dave followed through with the risk he needed to take—the risk he had to take three times—he overcame his fear of failure. That's a wonderful testimony of courage and resilience. But the greatest testimony to Dave's change in perception is that his increase in free time doubled his productivity. But that was only the first year. By the end of his second year with an assistant, his income had exploded by 500 percent.

Needless to say, some risks are worth taking.

THE PRODUCTIVE PERSPECTIVE

The only people reading this book—people like you—are those who are at least hoping that there is a better way, those who want to improve—even if they're already doing well. Some had already acknowledged their failure before beginning to read and are merely seeking advice. Others have just pinpointed their failures throughout the course of these pages. The only people that *aren't* reading this book are those who are too stubborn to admit or too obtuse to care that they are unproductive with their time. Who do you think is being more productive? Those who have sought to face their inefficiencies and improve? Or those who are still justifying their long days?

The answer is obvious. And that's because those who are brave enough to face their failures understand that to be successful—to continually increase productivity—you have to risk failure. Picking up this book was a risk, and I hope you feel it was worth taking. If we open our eyes, we begin to see that risk is in the very essence of anything worth having. And that includes more freedom with our time.

Take a look at the differences between the risk taker and the risk maker and for each description ask yourself, *does this save or steal time?*

The Risk Taker	The Risk Maker
Pursues dreams	Pacifies dreams
Aspires for greater success	Aspires for greater security
Is courageous	Is cautious
Thinks about succeeding	Thinks about not failing
Is a pioneer	Is a plodder
Is resilient	Is resistant
Is tenacious	Is timid

The differences between the two are many, but the gist of their disparity comes down to their titles. One takes risks because he understands it's the only way to create greater productivity. The other makes risks by avoiding failure and thus remains unproductive and increases the likelihood of regret.

In the seven previous chapters, I've asked you to give up some tasks that may not be easy for you to release. I've asked you to create some boundaries with your work time that will buck against your normal routine. I've asked you to break some unproductive habits. In short, I've asked you to take some risks with your career that may scare you or make you want to shy away and do nothing. But what I want you to see is that risk of failure is no reason to shy away from taking these steps. In fact, the whole teaching process of this book has been using failure to train you how to succeed.

We've been caught in time traps—we've been stuck in the grip of time-wasting routines. But instead of stewing in our failures, we've let them teach us how to improve. The only thing left to do is act on what we've learned. Hopefully, you've already begun.

THREE RISKS WORTH TAKING

The following are what I consider to be the top three risks worth taking in your sales career. I share these with you here because you are not only facing the decision to take them now; you will continue to face these risks after you've made the changes we've discussed—and I don't want failure to keep you from succeeding with your time.

Sure, these risks all carry with them a seed of failure, but with the right perspective, you won't ever go back to the unproductive, swamped salesperson you were.

1. *Develop an impossible vision.* The writer and poet T. S. Eliot once wrote, "Only those who risk going too far can possibly find out how far one can go."[2] What he was saying is that the only risks worth taking are those that elevate us higher than we are now—those that suggest we will receive something we've never received before. In our case, that means time. Isn't that what we've been talking about all along? If you want more time to sell—and live—than you've ever had before, you must stick your neck out. You must dare to have an impossible vision for your business that includes these three parameters:

◆ You can't accomplish it alone.

◆ It breeds fear and excitement simultaneously.

◆ It requires risk.

Take a chance and really dream here. Don't sell yourself short—no pun intended. Determine how productive you *ideally* want to be and how little you *ideally* would like to work. I'm not giving you permission to be unrealistic. Obviously, you will need to work more than one day a week to accomplish a decent level of success. You know what I mean. Once you've taken some time to dream, then set prospecting goals that will allow you to reach your sales goals, which will allow you to reach your income goal. Keep in mind that you have freed up a minimum of four hours a day to prospect and sell, and this represents a 167 percent increase in productive time based on the national average for salespeople (ninety productive minutes a day).

It's easy to determine how much more productive you can be by simply multiplying last year's prospecting, sales, and income numbers by 167 percent. With this formula, $50,000 in income becomes $83,500. If you use all that you have learned in solving the time traps and invest all eight hours selling, this increase goes to $334,000. Of course, productivity increase doesn't always translate proportionately into money increase, but the proportions are usually close. Besides, what I'm talking about is setting goals beyond that. Goals that are out of reach unless you get some help. Trust me, having a vision like this will only accelerate your success more.

2. *Become accountable to others.* In my book *High Trust Selling* I call this the Law of Leverage because it's the best way to maximize your potential.[3] There are three forms of leverage available to you:

- ◆ Personal leverage

- ◆ Associate leverage

- ◆ Professional leverage

And you need to employ them all in order to stretch your potential. Some may take an investment of your own money, but I have yet to meet a salesperson who invested in accountability—financially or emotionally—that didn't reap back more than he or she invested.

Let's break these forms of leverage down briefly so you can see how to employ them in your career.

Personal Leverage

This is merely setting up your own form of discipline that begins when you commit your impossible vision to paper, including the date you intend to realize it. A dream with a deadline provides positive pressure. It encourages you to eliminate excuses and take necessary, calculated risks. This is a good motivator when we need it, but to get to where we're going, we need more accountability than ourselves.

Associate Leverage

When you have another person hold you accountable for your vision and the steps that are required for you to get there, you gain even more leverage. It's one thing to be disciplined; it's another to have someone else in your business. This may not be comfortable for some of you, but remember, these are risky steps, and you have to take them if you are to ever maximize your time on and off the job.

The easiest way to enlist associate leverage is to ask a close friend or coworker to hold you accountable. If this person agrees, sit her down and share your impossible vision, including all the details. Then, when she is clear on the direction you are heading and has bought into your vision, set up a system by which your friend or coworker can hold you accountable. Don't just merely say, "Okay, so why don't you just ask me every now and then how I'm doing?" That isn't very effective. Set up something more formal, like a monthly dinner meeting or Saturday breakfast. Three coworkers put this form of leverage to use in 1992. At the time they were doing well but figured the accountability and friendly competition could only help. Five years later I interviewed them, and they had each more than tripled their productivity to the point that they accounted for 65 percent of their company's profit.

Regardless of who provides you associate leverage—whether it's your friend or coworker or spouse—the important thing to remember is that they must be people who take your goals seriously and find fulfillment in your fulfillment.

Professional Leverage

Whenever a salesperson approaches me at an event and shares his goals, I always ask him, "When?" because I feel my job as his "coach" is to hold him accountable. In many cases, attendees have spent their own money to come to the event, so I want them to leave with all the tools they need to succeed. This includes professional accountability. I've found that even when a person has associate leverage, there is more to be had with a coach. I believe the reason is that sales coaches can give you a fresh perspective on your job and, if you allow them, your life. Sometimes friends are too close to see a poor habit or attitude in us. Other times, coworkers empathize with our struggles and cannot be as forthcoming as they need to be. A coach can offer an unbiased, candid perspective on your career and help you tweak areas to maximum potential.

To this day, I still meet and talk on a regular basis with a few different men, some friends, some coaches, who each hold me accountable for different areas in my business and life. I can say without reservation that if I did not have the leverage they provide, I would not even be close to where I am today. I'd be working more than I should, spending less time with my family than I'd like, and still struggling to succeed. My accountability partners have made a huge difference, and so will yours.

3. *Set exceedingly high standards* so that failing to meet them will not have major consequences. This is a simple principle to understand, but one that's admittedly difficult to maintain. It takes guts. In order to set your standards so high that falling short isn't a major blunder, you have to have the ability to stick to your guns in some potentially difficult situations. This summer, I was faced with a very difficult situation in my family. It required a lot of my time, which cut dramatically into my ability to be productive at work. I had to move meetings and even cancel some commitments I had made. In fact, I fell behind on writing this book, but I kept at it when I could because I have standards I needed to uphold. And while I hate being late or having to back out of a commitment, I don't regret the decisions I've made to take care of my family. I cannot make up this time with them, and my partner and I can always write a book—I can always hold a meeting.

This particular risk isn't just about having high integrity; it's about leaving the office every day when you tell your family you will. It's about paying attention to your health despite the work you need to get done. It's about maintaining one face to every customer. It's about saying no when you must—even when saying yes is more lucrative. I could go on. The point is that in your new efforts to be successful, you will face challenges that don't arise when you're struggling to be mediocre.

Success presents its own adversaries, and if you're not prepared for them, you are in danger of squandering the time you free up. This is the last trap we must avoid. I call it the Party Trap, and it could be the most perilous trap of all.

Executive Summary

If past failures slow you down, then failure is a trap that steals time from today. But when you recognize that the only time you can do anything about is the moment you are in now, failure takes on a whole new meaning.

To overcome failure, we've been taught to be persistent, take initiative, be aggressive, and stick to it. Eventually we will gain the confidence to succeed more often. But the truth is that overcoming failure takes more than mental toughness and fervent initiative, more than an ability to avoid or ignore your setbacks. Overcoming failure takes perspective.

Salespeople with a healthy perspective of failure don't let their emotions go beyond disappointment. Once faced with the reality of failure, they adjust their attitude and resolve to take the necessary actions to learn from their mistakes and move forward with improved action. Ultimately, such salespeople end up in a better position than when they started. The paradox of failure is that while it's not the most productive path, it is often the most efficient teacher. The most productive salespeople understand this and as a result are willing to take the risks necessary to succeed—instead of shying away from the possibility of failure.

All risks carry within them a seed of failure, but with the right perspective, your failures will teach you what risks to take. The three most important risks are:

1. developing an impossible vision;
2. becoming accountable to others; and
3. setting exceedingly high standards so that failing to meet them will not have major consequences.

When you aren't afraid to take these three risks, you set yourself up for a level of success you may have never thought possible.

Chapter Nine

The Party Trap

Wasting Time Celebrating Success

Success is never final.

—WINSTON CHURCHILL

Try, not to become a man of success, but rather, try to become a man of values.

—ALBERT EINSTEIN

Yet when I surveyed all that my hands had done and what I had toiled to achieve, everything was meaningless, a chasing after the wind; nothing was gained under the sun.

—KING SOLOMON OF ISRAEL

We all went to Las Vegas to celebrate our success. We were the top-selling 10 percent in our company. We deserved it, right? Many years later I don't remember a lot from that trip, and most of what I do recall, I wish I could forget. I didn't have personal boundaries then. I knew this but couldn't change it—I was drowning in a cocktail of materialism and narcissism. I was losing control to alcohol and cocaine. Vegas was the last place I should have gone, but

I went because it was time to celebrate. After all, I had found out I was the top salesperson in my company.

I lost a lot of money in Vegas, but that could be replaced. What couldn't was my time. Not just that weekend, but the years I squandered in the name of success. That wasn't the only trip—it was just a typical one. There were others, over several years.

That first night in Las Vegas, I had enough Kamikazes to last a lifetime. I felt the alcohol for days. I was dressed in a facade of outward pleasure but suffering with inward pain. I was motivated to do something—I knew I was destroying myself—but no matter how hard I tried I couldn't change. What began as a little recreation was redefining who I was and erasing who I wanted to become. In essence, it was stealing the time my success had created.

EAT, DRINK, AND BE MERRY, FOR TOMORROW . . .

You know the rest. Tomorrow . . . we die. According to *The New Dictionary of Cultural Literacy*, the saying originated some four thousand years ago when Solomon, king of Israel, penned the following:[1]

> Then I realized that it is good . . . for a man to eat and drink, and to find satisfaction in his toilsome labor under the sun during the few days of life God has given him—for this is his lot.[2]

It's an inspiring passage, as if he's saying, "Go for it—live it up! Don't hold back. You only live once, so party hardy!" And many of us live by his proclamation. I certainly did. The problem is, we misunderstand the full meaning of his message.

To understand the significance of Solomon's words, you need to get to know him a little better.

Solomon was the firstborn son of King David, who was the second king of Israel, a man blessed by God, who amassed more victories and riches and fame than any king before him. Solomon's father was the giant slayer, the boy-king immortalized in marble by Michelangelo. It was in his grand stride that Solomon followed. And at first he did very well. In fact, he picked up where his father left off, and God blessed him even more. It is to Solomon that God said, "Ask for whatever you want me to give you."

Surprisingly, Solomon answered, "I am only a little child and do not know how to carry out my duties . . . So give your servant a discerning heart to govern your people and to distinguish between right and wrong."[3] Because Solomon asked for wisdom instead of wealth or power or honor for himself, God replied, "I will give you a wise and discerning heart, so that there will never have been anyone like you, nor will there ever be. Moreover, I will give you what you have *not* asked for—both riches and honor—so that in your lifetime you will have no equal among kings."[4]

Not a bad turn of events, is it? Solomon responded to God's offer humbly, and he was given the world on a golden platter, literally. "King Solomon was greater in riches and wisdom than all the other kings of the earth. The whole world sought audience with Solomon to hear the wisdom God had put in his heart. Year after year, everyone who came brought a gift—articles of silver and gold, robes, weapons and spices, and horses and mules."[5]

The weight of gold that Solomon received as gifts each year was twenty-five tons. All of the goblets and household articles in the palace were formed of pure gold. He amassed fourteen hundred chariots and twelve thousand horses; it is said that silver was considered of little value in his time, because it was as common as stones, and imported cedar was as common as the fig trees in the foothills.[6]

If there is one person of whom it can rightly be said, "He had it all," it is Solomon. If anyone should have understood the value of time, the art of making the most of his life, it was surely Solomon.

Maybe not. In the same passage as his misunderstood party procla-mation, we find these words:

Yet when I surveyed all that my hands had done and what I had toiled to achieve, everything was meaningless, a chasing after the wind; noth-ing was gained under the sun.[7]

After devoting more time than any man to the pursuit of wealth and knowledge and pleasure and honor, Solomon concluded that *success isn't what we think it is*. He had everything a person could want—more than anyone—and yet in the end he "hated life" (Ecclesiastes 2:17) because his pursuits—his use of time—ultimately left him empty, or better said, they left him unfulfilled. "Whoever loves wealth," he con-fessed, "is never satisfied with his income . . . Better one handful with tranquility than two handfuls with toil and chasing after the wind."[8]

Solomon's proclamation to eat, drink, and be merry is not what we've always assumed. In fact, it's not a proclamation as much as it is a warning. "For tomorrow we die" is not the phrase he chose, but it fits—in the context of Solomon's *complete* message, it reminds us that our time will be a complete waste if we don't understand how to really enjoy life—how to truly be successful.

You see, there is not *more* to success than we realize—there is *less*. And we must understand what that means if we are to reach a satis-fying conclusion about how we spend our time.

SUCCESS AND TIME

It's frightening how many salespeople live their lives by Solomon's decree and miss the significance of his statement. Solomon was a wise man, yes. It is said he was the wisest to ever live. But in the end he

admitted that his life was meaningless, because he used the abundance of his time to pursue things that didn't matter—"a chasing after the wind" is what he called it. "No man has power over the wind to contain it; so no one has power over the day of his death."[9]

Sound familiar?

I know many successful salespeople who are not yet wise enough to come to this same conclusion, and though they seem to succeed in sales, they never cease to squander the free time their success creates.

There's something you must realize about all this time stuff that we've been talking about. If you don't know what to do with the time that your sales success frees up, all that you've learned to this point is, to use Solomon's phrase, "utterly meaningless."[10]

Here's what I mean: if all you do is take the principles from the eight previous chapters and use them as a springboard to party harder, you'll end up like Solomon . . . or Howard Hughes . . . or me, a few years ago—chained down and limited by the time that should set you free.

I don't know where I'd be today if Sheryl hadn't intervened. She was my fiancée when I was at my worst—during my wasteful Vegas years. And while I didn't have the strength to change, she did.

She came to me one day and told me she was postponing our wedding until we could clean ourselves up. She, too, was struggling with cocaine and alcohol, but she was wiser and more courageous than I. She understood that "until death do us part" would be a present reality if we didn't begin using our success for something more than temporary pleasure. In essence, she understood that our misuse of success was devaluing, even diminishing, our time.

Success works hand in hand with time. Success should *appreciate* the value of your time; it should give you *more* time to spend on the things in your life that you value outside your job. And if you carry out all that we've discussed thus far, you will reap more time to do just that. But there's one caveat to success: if you're caught in the Party Trap like so many sales professionals, success will actually depreciate the value of your time. Unchanged, this pattern will eventually take back the time it once freed up.

If you don't know what I mean, consider the last time you tried to work after partying the night before. How was your productivity? And that's just the short-term effect. When it becomes a lifestyle, it's a different story.

Over the long term, the Party Trap will kill you—not figuratively—literally. Sadly, I've known salespeople of whom this was true.

Success is not something to be taken lightly. In fact, the way you handle success is just as important as how you handle failure.

THE PARADOX OF SUCCESS

In the last chapter we discussed how sales failure—though it saps your time initially—can actually shorten your learning curve and boost your productivity, if perceived in the right light. In short, the value of your selling time can be increased by failure if you have the right perception of and reaction to it.

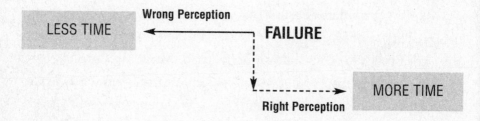

Success works in a similar way.

Your perception of success has the power to enhance or diminish the value of your time. By improving your sales skills and managing your tasks well—something you've learned to do in this book—you will free up more time on and off the job; this is the reward of success. You know what to do with the time you've freed up on the job: spend more time selling. What you do with the time you've freed up off the job is another story—that's where many salespeople lose control all over again.

The paradox of success is that if you invest your freed-up time in the wrong things—specifically, in the things that don't ultimately promote your highest values—your success can actually take more time from your life than it gives.

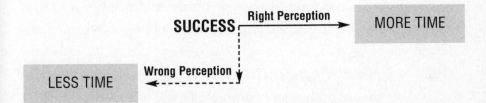

I recently shared this truth with a group of clients at a large national bank, and one approached me afterward to tell me about his father. Apparently, the man squandered his money and time foolishly for decades, and now, at sixty-five, the age when many men are playing a daily round of golf in Florida or Arizona, he's still living paycheck to paycheck with many regrets for what could have been.

I'm not saying that retirement or golf or year-round warm weather is the ultimate reward of success. Nor am I saying they should be your highest values. What I'm saying is that because this man's father misused his success for so many years, he's now running out of time to enjoy the life he never had.

SUCCEEDING WITH SUCCESS

Falling into the Party Trap happens subtly and, for many, somewhat innocently. We achieve a certain level of success and then . . .

- We lease a new car.
- We purchase new homes.
- We dine at fancier restaurants.
- We revamp our wardrobes.

These aren't bad things in moderation, and they are a fair return for sales success. Unfortunately, moderation isn't something we learn in sales training—nor is it an attribute we typically possess. Most salespeople are hard charging, full-throttle people. And just because we're not selling something, that doesn't mean we're gonna slow down.

The problem is that if you don't slow down and begin investing your success more thoughtfully, more purposefully, you will eventually come full scale and end up back where you were when you picked up this book—in a place where my client's father still is at sixty-five—wondering when your life passed you by.

On the other hand, if you decisively invest the time your success creates in the things you value most, sales achievement will truly breed life satisfaction. And after all, that's what we're after, isn't it? We don't just want to be a great salesperson—we want to live a great life. We want to enjoy the time we've been given.

Remember your definition of success from chapter two? What did you write? Take a moment to copy it here:

_____

_____

_____

_____

_____

If we're speaking from the heart, we have to admit that the idea of being successful brings with it a heightened anticipation that material comforts and temporary pleasures won't fulfill. If we're honest, the things we really desire from success aren't superficial—they are soulful, emotional, heartfelt longings. Sometimes you have to go deeper than your initial definition of success to realize what's really there. If you haven't yet, do it now. Take an honest look at your definition, and if it still has a superficial feel to it, ask yourself, *why do I want those things?* That question will get to the heart of your truest definition of success. There you might find the desire to spend more time with family, to go on great adventures with friends, to see the world and experience new cultures, to fall in love, to actively pursue a hobby or a dream you've always had, or to give more time to a cause that you're passionate about. Really, now—what are you feeling as I suggest these things? Don't you long for something deeper than material and financial gain? If so, then there's something more we must do with the time our success gives than merely eat, drink, and be merry.

King Solomon's conclusions about life were simple but profound, and I believe they give us great insight into the six areas in which we must consistently invest the time our success creates in order to avoid the laments of the Party Trap—to avoid his same regrets.

THE SIX MOST IMPORTANT INVESTMENTS FOR YOUR FREE TIME

#1 – Health

"Wine is a mocker and beer a brawler," said Solomon. "Whoever is led astray by them is not wise" (Proverbs 20:1). Something I learned in my bouts with cocaine and alcohol is that nothing steals your time quicker than poor health habits. Just think how much a little cold slows you down. When you add something more invasive, the effects multiply quickly. The four most common dependencies that affect your overall health are:

◆ alcohol

◆ nicotine

◆ food (overeating)

◆ caffeine

According to a national health survey, about 48 percent of adults consume alcohol regularly; 22 percent smoke; 58 percent are over-weight (22 percent are obese);[11] and about 30 percent of coffee drinkers claim to need it to function each day.[12] Obviously, each affects our health, which in turn devalues our ability to make the most of our time.

How much does it devalue our time? From a daily perspective we can only approximate, but it is fairly obvious that hangovers, smoke breaks, constant snacking, and frequent trips to the coffeemaker and bathroom all cut into our productivity during the course of a workday. Where your overall time is concerned, the short-term effects you experience (in less than a year of use) from these dependencies are ulcers, malnutrition, bad breath, immune deficiency, frequent colds, migraines, dehydration, skin problems, insomnia, anxiety, lack of energy, urinary tract infections, and diarrhea. Fun stuff, isn't it? Generally speaking, the long-term effect of dependence in these areas is a shorter life (except for caffeine, for which there is currently insufficient research). These probably are things you already know; but the correlation I want you to make is that if you don't take care of your body, your time is not maximized. That begins when you get a handle on what you consume. But that's not all. To truly enlarge the value of your time, you must take a proactive approach to health.

Several years ago, I remember looking at a photo of myself standing shirtless and proud in front of a new car I had purchased. I was disgusted at how bad I looked. Caught in the Party Trap, I had not only become an addict, but I had put on over forty pounds of fat. The sight of that picture thrust me onto a new path that has kept me full of energy and able to truly live out every one of my days. Here are the five simple steps that will help you do the same.

1. *Eliminate your intake of nicotine, and moderate your consumption of alcohol.* I know there are studies that indicate certain forms of alcohol are good in moderation, and that's fine if you want to go that route. However, it's easiest to eliminate the temptation altogether, because moderation often leads to indulgence very easily.

2. *Limit your intake of caffeine to no more than two cups of coffee a day* (studies show that anything more than this is potentially hazardous to your body). I began drinking lots of water. Studies show that two eight-ounce glasses of water in the morning and four to six more throughout the day can do more to increase your energy levels, improve your sleep patterns, and maintain your body's health than anything else.

3. *Begin exercising every day.* I keep it fresh by changing up what I do on a weekly basis, from biking to jogging to swimming to weights. This is important, as one of the biggest deterrents to a disciplined fitness routine is monotony. Don't let yourself get into a rut.

4. *Make a list of the foods you will no longer eat.* Don't go overboard with this—you want it to be something you can easily remember. You know what your Achilles heels are. If you want to optimize your energy, eliminate the foods that are dragging you down, and consume more energy-rich foods that are high in protein and fiber.

5. *Put yourself on a strict sleeping routine*. Okay, I know this sounds old-fashioned, but it really makes a difference. I travel a lot, so one of the things I have to constantly watch out for is jet lag. If I do not keep my body on a regimented sleeping routine, I lack the energy and mental capacity to enjoy my free time. "How long will you lie there?" asked Solomon. "A little sleeping, a little slumber ... and poverty will come on you like a bandit"[13] I'm a firm believer that when you give your body the food and exercise it needs, you will not feel the need to oversleep. And if you're using your time wisely, you will not need to undersleep to stay afloat.

#2 – Financial Fitness

"Go to the ant, you sluggard; consider its ways and be wise! It has no commander, no overseer or ruler, yet it stores its provisions in summer and gathers its food at harvest."[14] The statistics are staggering. According to the Social Security Administration, if you were to follow one hundred people from age twenty-five to sixty-five, you would find that:

◆ nineteen have died.

◆ fifteen will have incomes exceeding $30,000.

◆ sixty-six will have incomes less than $30,000.[15]

The statistics reflect the overall neglect of most people with regard to financial fitness. According to the Lincoln Financial Group, three of the top five reasons people suffer from poor financial fitness are:

1. lack of financial guidance;

2. poor investment choices; and

3. procrastination in starting a savings plan.[16]

As a child I learned several money-management principles from my parents, and though I didn't follow them while I was partying my life away, I have kept them as rules since stepping out of that trap. They have eliminated stress from my time and replaced it with security. This keeps my time alone or with others at the highest quality.

1. *Spend less than you make.* Open an account that you only use for your spending budget. Brent and his wife have a separate bank account for this. At the beginning of each month, the money allocated for their personal expenses is deposited into this separate account, creating a definitive end to what they can spend.

2. *Don't buy something unless you can afford to pay cash* (except for a nonde-preciating asset like a home). I know it's a temptation to put something on a card when more money is coming, but don't do it. Spend only *your* money, not the bank's.

> Spend only your money, not the bank's.

3. *Pay off your credit cards in full every month.* This applies only if you are using your card for monthly expenses in order to obtain travel miles. Otherwise, you shouldn't be using your cards.

4. *Put at least 10 percent of every dollar you make into an interest-earning savings account.* The interest will be low, but if you plan to leave it in there, you might as well make a few bucks on it.

5. *Give at least 10 percent of every dollar you make back to God.* By this I mean, invest your money in others through a church or charity.

This may not be your thing, but I guarantee you that this step will be the best investment you will make with your money.

6) *Set your own social status.* Don't get stuck trying to keep up with a certain social status that doesn't fit your budget. Buy the things that you can *afford* with the sales success you achieve—not what you or others think you *deserve.*

These are simple principles, I admit. But few live by them, and as a result, they spend more time than they should stressing and scrambling to make ends meet. There are not many things that make your free time more soothing than financial stability. (As a side note here, teach your kids early. My boys are still quite young—eight and seven—but every week when they get their weekly "paycheck," they have to put 10 percent into their God envelope, 10 percent into their savings envelope, and 80 percent into their spending envelope. This teaches them how to make financially fit choices early in life.)

#3 – Relationships

"Again I saw something meaningless," Solomon wrote. "There was a man all alone; he had neither son nor brother. There was no end to his toil . . . Two are better than one . . . Though one may be overpowered, two can defend themselves. A cord of three strands is not quickly broken."[17] Solomon was talking about family and friends. A person is to be pitied, he said, without someone to share his or her time with. On the other hand, there is strength, as the saying goes, in numbers. And there is beauty in sharing the best moments in our lives with people we love and enjoy.

Relationships grow more meaningful in proportion to the time we invest in them. "Closeness," said author John Drake, "doesn't happen if our time together occurs only when we get everything else done. Intimacy must be one of the things to be done."[18]

There are four types of relationships we should all invest our free time in if we are to reap the full benefits of sharing life with others:

1. *Modeling relationships.* Whom do you know that you respect and admire? Who maintains their standards and a level of integrity that you would like to emulate? Seek out these people and ask them if you can schedule regular meetings (maybe once a month) in order to learn from them. Don't be shy; if these people are as great as you think they are, they should be excited to add value to you.

2. *Mentoring relationships.* There's much to be said about investing in others in order to grow ourselves, but the true test of our knowledge and experience is our ability to pass it on to others. Besides, there is little more fulfilling than pouring our lives into another's and seeing that person bloom.

3. *Accountability relationships.* In Chapter 8 we discussed the importance of accountability partners in your career; but they are equally valuable outside of your work. What is it that you desire to accomplish outside of work? What do you dream about doing with your time once it's freed up? Once you know the answers, ask those people already helping you reach your work goals to hold you accountable for your personal goals and standards as well. They already know you and can offer you fresh ideas to help you maintain a schedule that allows you to meet both. "Many advisers," wrote Solomon, "make victory sure."[19]

4. *Intimate relationships.* Where would we be without those we love and who love us? I won't say much here except that we cannot do without

these people in our lives. Without intimate relationships grounded in love and mutual admiration, our free time is less than half as joyful and meaningful as it could be. What would life be without others? "Take away love," Robert Browning wrote, "and our earth is a tomb."[20]

#4 –Knowledge

"Blessed is the man," concluded Solomon, "who finds wisdom, the man who gains understanding, for she is more profitable than silver and yields better returns than gold. She is more precious than rubies; nothing you desire can compare with her. Long life is in her right hand; in her left hand are riches and honor. Her ways are pleasant ways, and all her paths are peace."[21] There are three ways that we can all invest our time in order to receive the best and most robust return in knowledge.

- *Read voraciously.* "Drink deep of great books," said John Wooden. Nothing furthers your knowledge more than books. I mentioned in chapter four that a great way for you to invest in your business is to make every other book you read something that helps you professionally. With the other books I recommend that you do what a friend does. She picks a topic that she's interested in and, for one year, reads everything she can on that topic. She's now well learned in French history, interior decorating, culinary arts, art history, and architecture—not to mention many other things. Talk about a great conversationalist!

- *Travel.* Get out more. Really. There's so much more you can learn about people, cultures, history, and life in general by spending time in places other than your hometown. There are lessons to be learned if only you'll get in the car or hop on a plane or train. Brent tells me that he and his wife plan to teach their children history and social studies by traveling to the places and letting them experience them firsthand. I think that's a great idea.

◆ *Take up new hobbies.* Do things you wouldn't normally do. Take up hang gliding or running 5Ks or kayaking in a lake or river nearby. Sheryl and I took up scuba diving several years ago, and now one of our favorite events every year is choosing a new place to dive. We read up on where we're going and always end up learning so much from our new experiences. I have learned to snowboard and love it. Wakeboarding is next. The boys and I are learning how to surf and motocross. Sheryl is cross-country skiing. What are you interested in doing? Try it out this year, and you'll not only learn something more about that topic, you'll learn a great deal about yourself in the process.

#5 – Purpose

This is undoubtedly the single most important investment of your free time. A person who has not sought out her purpose is like a ship without a sail. "The purposes of a man's heart are deep waters," said Solomon, "but a man of understanding draws them out."[22]

In order to make your time matter, you cannot ignore the question, *why am I here?* The fact that we want to know the answer indicates one thing: we were made for something more than just passing time. I challenge you to invest deep into this area—"draw out" your purpose—because ultimately, it is the root of every motive and desire you have. Read books on the topic of purpose, research what the Bible has to say about it, and ask others how they came to know their purposes. Most of all spend time in prayer.

Something I do on a regular basis is get away from the hustle and bustle of work and get alone. I go through a series of questions that help me continually focus the pursuits of my days on those few things that make up my life purpose. I recommend that you get alone, free of distractions, once a month to complete this exercise in order to continually clarify your answer to the *why* question. The most important thing is that you regularly invest your free time in this endeavor so that you will never again wonder where your best years went. Below are the questions I ask myself during my purpose-investment time:

- *Do I have confidence in my pursuits?*

- *Are my pursuits making use of my God-given abilities?*

- *Are my pursuits making others' lives better?*

- *Do I have any distractions in my life that are keeping my time from being truly maximized? How can I eliminate them?*

- *Will I be glad of my pursuits a year from now?*

- *Do I have any regrets from last month? How can I avoid those actions in the future?*

- *What is my greater purpose?*

- *Are the pursuits I am choosing to invest my time in each day fulfilling my greater purpose?*

- *How can I better invest my time so that what I desire for my future is possible?*

There's no magic number of questions that you should ask. The point is to get to the heart of your time struggles—to do your best to understand the gaps between how you are currently spending your time and how you should be spending your time. Success often gets us way off track if we don't stop and consider this.

But more than that, the goal is to determine what it is you want from your time. That question left unanswered can send you on a lifelong wild goose chase. I know plenty of very successful people (financially speaking) who are still chasing that ever-elusive bird. And you know what? They won't ever catch it. They might as well be chasing the wind beneath its wings.

On the other hand, when you know what you want from your time, the best path for your hours and your days becomes much clearer—and much more exhilarating, I might add. Once you know what your time is for, the only thing left to do is begin using it to that end.

It's an enchanting place to be—realizing the power you have to change the course of your own history. How will your story read five, ten, twenty years from now? Have you ever thought about that?

TIME IS AN OPEN BOOK

Imagine you are a writer, and an anonymous source has hired you to write a masterpiece. The topic and title are unknown; you've only been told that you should expect to receive more information in the mail—research information, you're guessing, that will explain the details.

The mail arrives one day, and with it a manila package. You open it and discover an attractive book bound in soft, chocolate leather, and a note. You open the note at once. It's only one sentence and reads:

THIS IS YOUR STORY TO WRITE HOWEVER YOU DESIRE.

You finger through the pages and find that every one is blank, except for a small inscription in the middle of the first page. It's your name, and beneath it, the current year with a long dash next to it—the final year yet to be determined.

Freeing up your time is like that. It's like being given a book of blank pages and asked to write your own story from start to finish, one day at a time, beginning today. What story will you tell? Who will help you write it? Who are the other characters? Is it a romance or an adventure? Maybe it's a bit of both. Whatever you decide, it's your book now, and the pen is in your hand. Don't be afraid to write from your heart. "It is the wellspring of life," said Solomon.[23] And if time is what life is made of, well, then, the key to making the most of your time is already written on the pages of your heart.

EXECUTIVE SUMMARY

Solomon's party proclamation to eat, drink, and be merry is not what we've always assumed. In fact, it's not a proclamation—it's a warning. "For tomorrow we die," is not the phrase he chose, but it fits: it reminds us that our time will be a complete waste if we don't understand how to *truly* enjoy life—how to really be successful.

After devoting more time than any man to the pursuits of wealth, knowledge, pleasure, and honor, Solomon concluded that *success isn't what we think it is*. He had everything a person could want—more than anyone in history—and yet in the end he "hated life" (Ecclesiastes 2:17), because his pursuits—his use of time—ultimately left him unfulfilled. "Whoever loves wealth," he confessed, "is never satisfied with his income . . . Better one handful with tranquility than two handfuls with toil and chasing after the wind" (Ecclesiastes 8:8).

You see, there is not *more* to success than we realize—there is *less*. And we must understand what that means if we are ever to reach a satisfying conclusion about how we spend our time.

Success works hand in hand with time. Success should *appreciate* the value of your time; it should give you *more* time to spend on the things in your life that you value outside your job. If you carry out all that we've discussed thus far, you will reap more time to do just that. But there's one caveat to success: if you're caught in the Party Trap, success will actually depreciate the value of your time. Unchanged, this pattern will eventually take back the time it once freed up, leaving you with empty regrets.

To avoid this unenviable plight, begin investing the time your success frees up in the following six areas:

1. Health
2. Financial fitness
3. Relationships
4. Knowledge
5. Purpose

When you know what you want from your time, the best path for your hours and your days becomes much clearer—and much more exhilarating. Once you know what your time is for, the only thing left to do is begin using it to that end.

Chapter Ten

Freedom

What will you do without freedom? Will you fight?

—WILLIAM WALLACE IN *BRAVEHEART*

As I sit on the rugged cliffs perched above the edge of the Pacific, my mind is quiet. The scene before me is still, as though its artist waits for me to take in every last detail of its beauty. Although I'm some twenty feet above the ocean, I think I can feel the touch of the cool tide as it reaches up the sand, then slowly withdraws into the blue.

In moments like these, you have time to think about more than today. I am rewinding the tape of my life, and instinctively I push play. There they are, in Technicolor, on the screen of my mind, the memories I cherish most—those critical moments where I followed my heart, and not necessarily my head. Dinner at a restaurant an hour away, because it was important to a good friend. Midday hooky with my boys at the beach. A plane ride home from a speaking engagement a day early so I could kiss my wife good night. An all-nighter to finish a writing project. An early breakfast with an event attendee who needed someone to listen. All moments when I wasn't necessarily making a better living, but I was absolutely living my best life.

As the movie reels to an end, I press pause. I realize I have found my heart. I have found that place where time makes sense. And it's in that place that I long to stay. But time moves on despite me.

The days pass. The vacation ends. The memories still linger, but only like a morning mist now. Back to work, time is moving more quickly than I'd like. Business has reemerged, urgencies have crept back in, and I long for another magical moment, another hit of something that warms my soul.

I am sitting in my office now. The day has been planned for weeks. The writing of this book is coming to an end. The research is finished, the resources are before me, and the cursor pulses impatiently. I close the office door and attempt to clear my head.

I forgot one thing, however, and that was to turn off my cell phone—it rings. "Hi, honey," my wife, Sheryl, says cheerfully. "The boys would love to go to IHOP with you this morning. Do you think you can swing it?"

The moment awaits my decision. *Do I or don't I?* I'd feel guilty if I didn't, but I have work I have to get done. Then from somewhere inside, deep inside, I hear another voice. *What is the value of time?* it asks. *Money or life?*

My head is telling me I cannot spare a minute—I need to get a lot of writing done today. My heart has a different message. It's reminding me that my boys are more important to me than my work. It's convincing me that even though I will be giving up an hour or more of writing time, five minutes with my boys is more valuable. They won't be little for long, and they won't always want to go to IHOP with their daddy. A time will come when they'll have agendas of their own, and their lives won't revolve around Mom and Dad. One day, they will have their own families, and I will long for an opportunity to spend an hour with them, chatting and laughing over a big stack of syrup-drenched flapjacks. *Yes, even though I love what I do for a living, this time with my boys, this is what I truly long for. If I really need it, I can make up an hour of writing later, when they're asleep.*

The decision is made, and fifteen minutes later the four of us are sitting at our table in IHOP, laughing like the best of friends, as we always do.

I have found my heart again, and it is full.

MAGICAL MOMENTS

I'm now on a little island called Nevis in the West Indies. And as the day draws to a close, I'm sitting on the beach, staring at the Caribbean, enjoying the salty-sweet breeze and cheering the waves as they lap gently onto the white sand. If I squint toward the horizon, the sea and sky fuse together into one giant sapphire canvas waiting for the next sunset to be painted. *It has been a good week*, I think to myself. But little do I realize what is in store.

As I close the weeklong seminar the next morning, an announcement is made to the people in the audience: the next day is my birthday. I am surprised and a little embarrassed at the announcement, as I had hoped that detail would slip under the radar. But the damage has been done. A cake is rolled out from the kitchen, a song is sung (with all the harmony of a flock of crows), and a big smile comes over my face when I realize my wife is behind it all. Then a second announcement is given: there is a video to watch. I think perhaps an anthology of the history of my company, but how shallow of me to go there. Instead, I sit speechless and teary-eyed as I witness a thirteen-minute masterpiece featuring five years of magical moments with my two boys. Sheryl has assembled the video as a birthday wish from my boys who could not make the trip with us. The video is titled "Welcome to Our Journey of Fun with Daddy."

The song accompanying the video is called "Before You Grow" by

Dennis Scott and Timmy Tappan. Its lyrics tell of a parent confessing to his small child that he'd like to become the best of friends, to get to know him well, before time passes quickly and he's full grown.[1]

The words penetrate my heart as the tape continues to roll. *This is what my life is all about!* I say to myself, as I watch my boys dancing and laughing as they run from ocean waves. *These are the moments that make me feel alive! This is the value of time.*

As the video concludes, I wipe my eyes once more. My heart feels healthy and strong—the way it should—and I want the feeling to last forever.

We all have them. Magical moments. Moments when life seems to work just right, when our hearts are complete and we feel completely alive. Sometimes we're with our families. Other times we're with close friends or only our spouses or a significant other. And sometimes we're alone in an inspiring, idyllic place. For some of us, the moments only occur rarely. For others, they occur more often. But regardless of the frequency, one thing is for sure: we never want to lose the feeling those moments provide, because they remind us that time is on our side when we know how to use it.

In his book *The Journey of Desire*, author John Eldredge explained:

> There is a secret set within each of our hearts . . . It is the desire for life as it was meant to be . . . You may not always be aware of your search, and there are times when you seem to have abandoned looking altogether. But again and again it returns to us, this yearning that cries out for the life we prize . . .
>
> The greatest human tragedy is to give up the search. Nothing is of greater importance than the life of our deep heart. To lose heart is to lose everything. And if we are to bring our hearts along in our life's journey, we simply must not, we cannot, abandon this desire . . .

The clue as to who we really are and why we are here comes to us through our heart's desire. But it comes in surprising ways, and often goes unnoticed or is misunderstood. Once in a while life comes together for us in a way that feels good and right and what we've been waiting for. These are the moments in our lives that we wish could go on forever. They aren't necessarily the "Kodak moments," weddings and births and great achievements. More often than not they come in subtler, unexpected ways, as if to sneak up on us.

Think of times in your life that made you wish for all the world that you had the power to make time stand still. Are they not moments of love, moments of joy? Simple moments of rest and quiet when all seems to be well. Something in your heart says, *Finally, it has come. This is what I was made for!²*

WHAT IS PRICELESS?

One of the most memorable ad campaigns of the last decade includes the "Priceless" MasterCard ads that always end with, "Some things money can't buy. For everything else, there's MasterCard." You've no doubt seen them. The ads usually feature a happy couple, or some family members, or a group of friends who spend specific dollar amounts on items like, *Two tickets to a baseball game: $24*, or *Four plane tickets to Paris: $3,000*, or *Dinner at your favorite restaurant: $149*. And as each dollar amount is listed with its accompanying scene, we begin to piece together an event that is taking place. Then the ads conclude with a scene like a father and son cheering at a baseball game, or a group of friends laughing over dinner, or a couple walking hand in hand along a white sandy beach, all experiencing a memorable, significant moment in their lives. And then comes the tag line: *Spending your 40th birthday with the one you* *love: Priceless.* We watch, and as soon as that line is spoken, we feel it—that warm feeling deep inside. Maybe we even get a little glassy-eyed. Our hearts are moved because we, too, have experienced similar moments—priceless moments. The only thing that is priceless, after all, is time.

What would *your* MasterCard ad look like? What are the magical moments in your life, when everything seemed to come together and your heart was full? Where were you? What were you doing? Maybe you were with close friends, trekking all over Europe. Or eating and laughing for hours at your favorite restaurant. Or driving up the coast with the one you love, without an agenda, the top down and warm wind in your hair. Maybe you were someplace with your kids . . . enjoying someplace they love, like Disneyland, or a big-league baseball game. Maybe you were with your spouse or special someone . . . cuddling on a picnic blanket, staring at a mountain sky full of stars. Or maybe away from it all in a log cabin with nothing but a fireplace, a warm blanket, and each other. Maybe the moments weren't planned, and they just snuck up and grabbed hold of your heart unexpectedly. As Eldredge points out, they happen quite often that way. It's our heart's way of saying, *I'm still here! This is the time I long for. Please don't ignore it. I'm showing you what makes me alive.*

There are no wrong answers to how or when or why heartfelt moments happen in our lives, because only we can sense what truly fills our hearts. We know when time has been well spent, because our hearts tell us. And the only difference between those who experience more of those moments and the rest is how they deal with the desires of their deepest hearts. There are only two options you have: either you continue to strive after them, arranging for more time to do what you desire, or you grow complacent and resolve to be content spending time on something less than what your heart desires. Enough of this and your true desires eventually go dormant.

WE ONLY REGRET WASTED TIME

In the national best seller *Tuesdays with Morrie*, author Mitch Albom recounts a discussion with his dying mentor on their third Tuesday meeting. The discussion centered on regrets, and it teaches us a powerful lesson about the critical importance of following our true hearts in the time we have now, before it's too late.

The first time I saw Morrie on "Nightline," I wondered what regrets he had once he knew his death was imminent. Did he lament lost friends? Would he have done much differently? Selfishly, I wondered if I were in his shoes, would I be consumed with sad thoughts of all that I had missed? Would I regret the secrets I had kept hidden?

When I mentioned this to Morrie, he nodded. "It's what everyone worries about, isn't it? What if today were my last day on earth?" He studied my face, and perhaps he saw an ambivalence about my own choices. I had this vision of me keeling over at my desk one day, halfway through a story, my editors snatching the copy even as the medics carried my body away.

"Mitch?" Morrie said.

I shook my head and said nothing. But Morrie picked up on my hesitation.

"Mitch," he said, "the culture doesn't encourage you to think about such things until you're about to die. We're so wrapped up with egotistical things, career, having enough money, meeting the mortgage, getting a new car, fixing the radiator when it breaks—we're involved in trillions of little acts just to keep going. So we don't get into the habit of standing back and looking at our lives and saying, *Is this all? Is this all I want? Is something missing?"*[3]

Isn't there a life that you've been searching for all of your days? I'm not asking if you have some happiness in your life, or if you want to be successful, or even if you have more good days than bad—I'm asking if your life is the life you've always wanted.

Or is there still a yearning deep down for something else, something more, something greater? The truth is, we all have the yearning to an extent. It remains in our deepest selves, and though we often cannot put words to it, the longing seems to follow us throughout our days, attempting to guide us to spend our time in certain ways. Will you heed its advice?

We *are* designed for something more. Something more fulfilling, more rewarding, more enriching, more exciting. And often our hearts are crying out for that missing element, that next step to achieving more of the freedom we desire.

> We are designed for something more. Something more fulfilling, more rewarding, more enriching, more exciting.

"It is only with the heart," asserted Antoine de Saint-Exupery, "that one can see rightly; what is essential is invisible to the eye."[4] Deep down, our hearts preserve the secret to our lives.

TIME AND THE SPIRITUAL HEART

Your spiritual heart is the epicenter, the soul of your most desired life. And like your physical heart, if neglected your spiritual heart will eventually stop beating, and your life will seem a dismal existence, an ambivalent passing of time until death. On the outside, you might continue to live a life of quiet desperation—going through the motions—but on the inside you will have expired, having given up your once-high hopes of a beautiful life.

The resulting realities of a starving spiritual heart are just as disturbing as those of a starving physical heart. Most common are feelings of confusion, dissatisfaction, sadness, loneliness, anger, and resentment, which eventually lead to harsher realities, like criminal activity, divorce, bankruptcy, depression, and, God forbid, even suicide. The health of your spiritual heart is serious business—maybe more serious than that of your physical heart.

Yet people still continue to suffer from spiritual heart dysfunction every year. Look at the statistics.

The majority of people are dissatisfied with . . .

Their marriages: The current divorce rate in United States is about 60 percent.

Their jobs: In a national survey conducted by *Fast Company* magazine, 77 percent of respondents (all professionals) indicated that if money were not an issue, they would either quit their jobs or dramatically reduce their hours.[5]

Their money: The same survey showed that the vast majority of respondents feel they don't make enough money to live a substantial, purposeful life. When asked to indicate the key factors that would help them achieve satisfaction and balance in their lives, 86 percent identified "making more money" as critical, and 70 percent of respondents said it would take no less than an extra $50,000 a year to achieve satisfaction and allow them to do what they really want to do.

Their lives: The article concluded with these thoughts:

For the moment—which is all that we can see clearly—most of us are prepared to embrace this precarious blend of wanting and having, of getting and spending, and to call it "balance." We believe that at some point, having "more" of something—more money, more self-knowledge—will change the game in a way that yields a new style of work, a new way of life, and a new sense of personal freedom. Then at last, we will have it all.

In another national survey conducted by the Barna Research Group, 50 percent of all Americans say they are still searching for meaning and purpose in life, and 60 percent say they are generally skeptical about their lives. In responding to the survey results, founder George Barna said the following:

> The common solution [for a dissatisfied life] is to keep busy and to stimulate ourselves with a variety of new experiences—that way we are not so likely to feel the pain of those fundamental holes in our lives. People have discovered that if they fill the gaps with commitments and excitement, then they're less prone to feel the emptiness of loneliness and aimlessness. Of course, that just prolongs the inner despair that eventually cannot be suppressed any longer.[6]

Unfortunately, like the physical hearts of so many, the spiritual hearts of millions are withering every year. Too many people are dying for tomorrow rather than living for today. In the end, they miss life altogether because they don't make the connection between heart and hope. Hope suggests to you there is a better tomorrow, while heart instructs you to do something about it today. Hope is backed by faith, and there's nothing wrong with that in and of

Too many people are dying for tomorrow rather than living for today.

itself. But heart is backed by action. Heart is the sure voice of hope that conveys to you what must be done with your time now in order to fulfill your truest desires.

If you are to reclaim the life you desire—on the job, at home—you must not ignore your heart's attempts to guide your time, even if what it's saying is contrary to what you're hearing in your head.

YOUR MOST NOBLE PURSUIT

In 1995, a film titled *First Knight* debuted and went somewhat unnoticed at the box office, due in large part to the huge success of another great film, *Braveheart*. *First Knight*, however, has since become a rental favorite. The film is a wonderful take on the age-old story of King Arthur (played by Sean Connery), Lady Guinevere (played by Julia Ormond), and Sir Lancelot (played by Richard Gere), and it provides a powerful illustration of the three characters' journeys to understand and follow the true desires of their hearts.

The story first introduces us to Lancelot, a rogue wanderer who is fearless and mysterious.

A narrator opens the movie with these words:

And then there was Lancelot, a wanderer who had never dreamed of peace or justice or knighthood. Times were hard. A man made his living any way he could. And Lancelot had always been good with a sword . . .

At face value, we take Lancelot for a man full of passion and adventure—a man who seizes the day and more. We are drawn to his unbridled, mysterious ways. But as we find out, there's more to Lancelot than meets the eye. Soon he meets King Arthur, who discerns that Lancelot is really masking his pain behind the facade of his tough exterior.

We pick up the story after Lancelot has just beaten the Gauntlet, a medieval obstacle course, which, to that point, had never been bested. Thoroughly impressed at Lancelot's feat, Arthur invites him in the castle to show him the famous Roundtable. As Lancelot leans on the table, he reads the circular inscription.

Lancelot: "In serving each other, we become free."

Arthur: That is the very heart of Camelot. Not these stones, timbers, towers, palaces. Burn them all, and Camelot lives on because it lives in us. It's a belief we hold in our hearts. [*Returns his sword to its sheath and exchanges a brief glance with Lancelot*] Well, no matter. Stay in Camelot; I invite you.

Lancelot: [*Laughing*] Thank you. But I'll be on the road again soon.

Arthur: Oh? What road?

Lancelot: Wherever chance takes me. I have no plans.

Arthur: So you believe that what you do is a matter of chance?

Lancelot: [*Confidently*] Yes.

Arthur: [*Pointing*] Well, at the end of that hallway there are two doors— one to the left and one to the right. How will you decide which door to take?

Lancelot: Left or right. Makes no difference. It's all chance.

Arthur: Then I hope chance leads you to the left because it's the only way out. [*Lancelot smiles, nods good-bye, and turns to leave*]

Arthur: Lancelot? [*Lancelot stops; turns to face Arthur as he continues speaking*] Just a thought . . . A man who fears nothing is a man who loves nothing. And if you love nothing, what joy is there in your life?

They are words that haunt Lancelot despite his efforts to shake them and remain true to his aimless ways. Words that eventually break through the thick wall suffocating his heart's deepest desires for companionship and a noble purpose. They are the words, in fact, that prompt Lancelot to eventually make his time matter for more than chance circumstances. In the end, a dying Arthur entrusts the kingdom to Lancelot whose heart has become the embodiment of Camelot.

Reclaiming Your Heart . . . and Your Time

Where is your heart discontented? What is missing in your life? Like Lancelot, are you masking your true desires behind a facade of good-looking pursuits? What is it that your heart is truly beating for? That's what your time is meant for.

"The heart," said Blaise Pascal, "has reasons which reason cannot understand." So don't be surprised if there are moments when what your heart is saying doesn't seem attainable or even practical. The battle between head and heart is lifelong. But you must learn to trust that it's the heart, as Thomas Carlyle said, "that sees before the head can see." It is only your heart, in other words, that holds the answers to the life you truly desire. It is your heart that reveals what makes time matter to you. It is your heart that shows you the way to true time freedom.

What new choices do you need to make in how you are using your time? No one can make new choices for you. Your choices are yours alone. They are the minutes of your days that either prohibit or provide life.

Take an honest inventory of your life. Is it a reflection of your uniqueness, your ardent desires—or are you on autopilot, just going through the motions, filling up time? Keeping your desk neat and paperwork filed, returning your phone calls, pleasing who needs to be pleased, paying your bills on time, saving for that big trip that you'll take one day when you have more time, and looking forward to retirement when you get old so then you can *really* enjoy life. Aren't you looking forward to something more than retirement? "If your memories of the past are greater than your dreams of the future," as my friend Bob Shank says, "you're already dead."

If a voice deep inside is still telling you there's something more, something better, something you're still longing for, something worth striving for and fighting for, then your heart is still beating and there is still time to do something about it.

Now is the time to act. Now is the time to live. Your future is not some far-off mystical dream. The look of your future is merely the culmination of how you most frequently spend your time. After all that we've said and done, I hope that you will spend it wisely today and every day hereafter.

That alone leads to freedom.

Notes

Chapter One: Chasing the Wind

1. Genesis 1:1, 3–5 reads, "In the beginning God created the heavens and the earth . . . And God said, 'Let there be light,' and there was light. God saw that the light was good, and he separated the light from the darkness. God called the light 'day,' and the darkness he called 'night.' And there was evening, and there was morning—the first day."

2. Marcia Hornok, "Psalm 23 Antithesis," originally published in *Discipleship Journal*, 60 (November, 1990).

Chapter Two: The Identity Trap

1. Barrie Greiff and Preston K. Munter, *Tradeoffs: Executive, Family, and Organizational Life* (New York: New American Library, 1980), as cited by John D. Drake, *Downshifting* (San Francisco: Berrett-Koehler Publishers, Inc., 2000), 9.

2. Al Gini, *My Job My Self: Work and the Creation of the Modern Individual* (New York: Routledge, 2001), 2.

3. "Bring Back the Eight-Hour Day," © Charlie King/Pied ASP Music-BMI. From the album *Inside Out*.

4. To paraphrase Joe Robinson in *Work to Live* (New York: The Berkley Publishing Group, 2003), 25.

5. Robinson, *Work to Live*, 20–21.

6. Ilene Philipson, *Married to the Job* (New York: The Free Press, 2002), 19–20.

7. Al Gini, *The Importance of Being Lazy* (New York: Routledge, 2003), 32.

8. Philipson, *Married to the Job*, 124, quoting Jerry Useem, *Fortune* magazine.

9. On page 56 Philipson is citing from an interview conducted by Arlie Hochschild in her book *The Time Bind: When Work Becomes Home and Home Becomes Work* (New York: Owl Books, 2001).

10. According to statistics provided by authors Jared Brenstein, Heather Boushey, and Lawrence Mishel in *The State of Working America 2002/2003* (New York: Cornell University Press, 2003).

11. Gini, *Being Lazy*. Gini is citing Benjamin Kline Hunnicutt, "A Fast-Paced Look at the Whirl and Flux of Modern Life," *Chicago Tribune*, September 19, 1999, Books.

12. Robinson, *Work to Live*, 18–19.

Chapter Three: The Organization Trap

1. According to studies conducted by our affiliate, Building Champions.

2. Used with permission from Building Champions © 2003.

3. Information on the Hoover Dam provided by www.usbr.gov/lc/hooverdam/. For more information on this incredible structure, please visit this site.

4. All figures based on a five-day week and a forty-six-week year.

Chapter Four: The Yes Trap

1. According to productivity expert David Allen in his book *Getting Things Done* (New York: Penguin Books, 2003).

2. Story shared by an anonymous contributor to the Monster.com Web-based archive titled *The Accidental Salesperson.*

3. National Sleep Foundation, public opinion survey "Sleep in America," www.sleepfoundation.org.

4. Robinson, *Work to Live.* Robinson is citing Joan Williams in her book *Unbending Gender: Why Family and Work Conflict and What to Do About It* (New York: Oxford University Press, 2001), 27–28.

5. National Sleep Foundation

6. I am indebted to my friend Brian Tracy for his research on these two surveys, which are reported in his book *Time Power* (New York: Amacom, 2004), 228–29.

7. For the full report titled "Missing Millions: How Companies Mismanage Their Most Valuable Resource" see www.proudfoot-plc.com/ and click on the link in the "Spotlight" box that allows you to view previous studies.

8. I am grateful to Brian Tracy and David Allen for their insight on using similar filing systems.

9. If you don't know how to set an auto-response for your e-mail address, an IT professional in your office or through your Internet provider can help you do this.

Chapter Five: The Control Trap

1. My description of the scene is an adaptation of two versions of *The Lord of the Rings: The Return of the King* (2003) screenplay offered by Noora at www.legomirk.com and a contributor to www.seatofkings.com. The story was originally written in book form by J. R. R. Tolkien in 1938 and was adapted for the screen by Peter Jackson, Fran Walsh, and Phillip Boyens.

2. John C. Maxwell, *The 17 Indispensable Laws of Teamwork* (Nashville: Thomas Nelson, 2000).

Chapter Six: The Technology Trap

1. William Hepworth Dixon, *The Story of Lord Bacon's Life* (London: John Murray, 1862).

2. Paul Andrews, "Saving Time No Longer a Tech Reality," *The Seattle Times*, October 20, 2003.

3. Visit www.KillingtheSale.com for more information or to purchase a copy of the book.

4. Jon Swartz, "Is the Future of E-mail Under Cyberattack?" *USA Today*, June 15, 2004.

5. According to a *WIRED* magazine news report titled "Viruses Cost Big Bucks," June 18, 1999. This report can be found at www.wired.com/news/technology/

6. As reported on *Entrepreneur* magazine's Web site, www.entrepreneur.com, in a piece titled "Viruses Cost Billions," April 23, 2003.

7. Paul Davidson, "Do-Not-Spam Registry Could Result in More Spam, FTC Says," *USA Today*, June 15, 2004.

8. Brad Stone, "Your Next Computer," *Newsweek*, June 7, 2004.

Chapter Seven: The Quota Trap

1. For the full report see the September, 2003 issue of the *Career Choices* newsletter on www.CareerPrep.com.

2. Erin Strout, "To Tell the Truth: Call It What You Like: A Fib, an Untruth, a Fabrication." "A new SMM survey reveals that nearly half of all salespeople may lie to clients. Are you creating a culture that promotes deception?" *Sales and Marketing Management*, July, 2002.

3. For a time-effective prospecting strategy, read chapters 9 and 10 in *High Trust Selling* (Nashville: Thomas Nelson Publishers, 2003).

Chapter Eight: The Failure Trap

1. Copyright 2003, Switchfoot. From their Platinum album *The Beautiful Letdown*, Columbia/Red INK, 2003. *Lyrics written by lead singer Jon Foreman.

2. John Cook, ed., *The Book of Positive Quotations* (Minneapolis: Fairview Press, 1997).

3. Visit www.HighTrustSelling.com for more information or to purchase a copy of the book.

Chapter Nine: The Party Trap

1. E. D. Hirsch Jr., Joseph F. Kett, and James Trefil, eds., *The New Dictionary of Cultural Literacy*, 3rd ed. (Boston: Houghton Mifflin Company, 2002).

2. Ecclesiastes 5:18.

3. 1 Kings 3:5, 7, 9.

4. 1 Kings 3:12–13, emphasis mine.

5. 1 Kings 10:23–25.

6. See 1 Kings 10:14–29.

7. Ecclesiastes 2:11–11.

8. Ecclesiastes 5:10; 4:6.

9. Ecclesiastes 8:8.

10. Ecclesiastes 1:2.

11. The "National Health Interview Survey" was published by the U.S. Dept. of Health and Human Services, the Centers for Disease Control and Prevention, and the National Center for Health Statistics, Hyattsville, MD, July, 2004.

12. Statistics from GlobalChange.com and are excerpted from Patrick Dixon, *The Truth About Drugs* (London: Hodder, 1998).

13. Proverbs 6:9–11.

14. Proverbs 6:6–8.

15. These statistics are as of 2000 and were first reported in my book *Wealth Strategies* (Nashville: W Publishing, 2000).

16. Information is based on an interview conducted in 2000 with Jeff Duncan, a top producer for Lincoln Financial.

17. Ecclesiastes 4:7–9, 12.

18. John D. Drake, Ph.D., *Downshifting* (San Francisco: Berrett-Koehler Publishers, Inc., 2000), 100.

19. Proverbs 11:14.

20. Cook, *Positive Quotations*.

21. Proverbs 3:13–17.

22. Proverbs 20:5.

23. Proverbs 4:23.

Chapter Ten: Freedom

1. "Before You Grow" written by Dennis Scott and Timmy Tappan © 1992, Act IV Music SESAC/Music Match Inc. BMI.

2. John Eldredge, *The Journey of Desire* (Nashville: Thomas Nelson, 2001), 1–3.

3. Mitch Albom, *Tuesdays with Morrie* (New York: Doubleday, 1997), 64–65.

4. Cook, *Positive Quotations*.

5. From the article titled "How Much Is Enough?" *Fast Company* magazine, July 1999.

6. Provided by the Barna Research Group online at www.barna.org.

About the Author

Todd Duncan is one of America's leading experts in the area of Sales and Life Mastery. His publisher, Thomas Nelson, calls him "an exciting combination of Zig Ziglar's energy and style, with John Maxwell's content."

Dr. John C. Maxwell says, "Todd just plain delivers the goods . . . and people's personal and financial lives are being tremendously and greatly impacted."

Todd Duncan has devoted the last twenty-three years to researching high-performance, successful people in all walks of business and life. His findings have been synthesized into one of the most powerful programs ever created on how to live a more meaningful, fulfilling, enriching, and profitable life.

Zig Ziglar says, "I know a little something about selling and success . . . and about motivating people to reach their goals. As I've watched Todd Duncan over the years, I've seen in him a lot of the same passion, the same spark, the same drive that has motivated me."

Todd's best-selling books and seminars have influenced millions of people. Of Todd's book *High Trust Selling*, Ken Blanchard says, "If you're serious about selling you must read this book. It's a breakthrough!" *High Trust Selling,* published by Thomas Nelson, is a *Wall Street Journal, Business Week, Los Angeles Times,* and Barnes and Noble business best-selling book.

The Duncan Group has its corporate office in Atlanta, Georgia. Todd and his wife, Sheryl, have two sons and live in La Jolla, California.

www.theduncangroup.com